MAD
COVER TO COVER

48 Years, 6 Months, & 3 Days of *MAD* Magazine Covers

By "The Usual
Gang of Idiots"

With Running Commentary
by Frank Jacobs

WATSON-GUPTILL PUBLICATIONS
a division of BPI Communications, Inc.
New York

ACKNOWLEDGMENTS

What can one say about *MAD*'s first four hundred covers? A great deal, as I found out in putting together this collection. And for that I'm indebted to several knowledgeable people.

MAD's co-editors, Nick Meglin and John Ficarra, supplied the lion's share of information. They surveyed forty-eight years of covers, singling out the ones warranting special attention and sharing a bounty of historical data and remembrances.

Former editor Al Feldstein recalled the cover-creating process as it was during *MAD*'s early years.

Grant Geissman, whose obsession with *MAD* is legendary, cleared up many details, a number of which dealt with the evolution of Alfred E. Neuman.

Artists Kelly Freas and Mort Drucker were generous with their time and thoughts, as were *MAD* stalwarts Sergio Aragonés, Duck Edwing, and Al Jaffee. Annie Gaines, as always, was of immeasurable help.

Special thanks also to Alison Hagge at Watson-Guptill and Jay Anning at Thumb Print.

Finally, I'm most grateful to Charlie Kochman who, as liaison between me and the *MAD* establishment, provided incalculable aid. His diligence and patience helped smooth the way in bringing this project to fruition.

FRANK JACOBS
April 1, 2000

Bill Gaines and Frank Jacobs.
Photo by Irving Schild (September 1977)

First published in 2000 by Watson-Guptill Publications
a division of BPI Communications, Inc.
770 Broadway, New York, NY 10003
www.watsonguptill.com

Library of Congress Cataloging-in-Publication Data

Mad : cover to cover : 48 years, 6 months & 3 days of Mad magazine covers / by the Usual Gang of Idiots ; with running commentary by Frank Jacobs.
      p.   cm.
  ISBN 0-8230-1684-6
     1. Mad (New York, N.Y. : 1958)—Illustrations. 2. Magazine covers—United States.
  3. American wit and humor, Pictorial. I. Jacobs, Frank. II. Mad (New York, N.Y. : 1958)
  NC974.4.M33 M33 2000
  741.6'52'0973—dc21

                                     00-040820

The principal typefaces used in the composition of this book were 10-point ITC Weidemann Book and 7-point ITC Bailey Sans Book.

Manufactured in the United States of America

First printing, 2000

1 2 3 4 5 6 7 8 9 / 08 07 06 05 04 03 02 01 00

Norman Mingo and Bill Gaines

For Watson-Guptill Publications:
Senior Acquisitions Editor: Candace Raney
Associate Editor: Alison Hagge
Production Manager: Ellen Greene
Marketing Manager: Ali Kokmen
Cover and interior design: Jay Anning, Thumb Print

For E.C. Publications:
Editors: Nick Meglin and John Ficarra (*MAD*)
Editor: Charles Kochman (Licensed Publishing)

In memory of Norman Mingo, pictorial godfather to Alfred E. Neuman

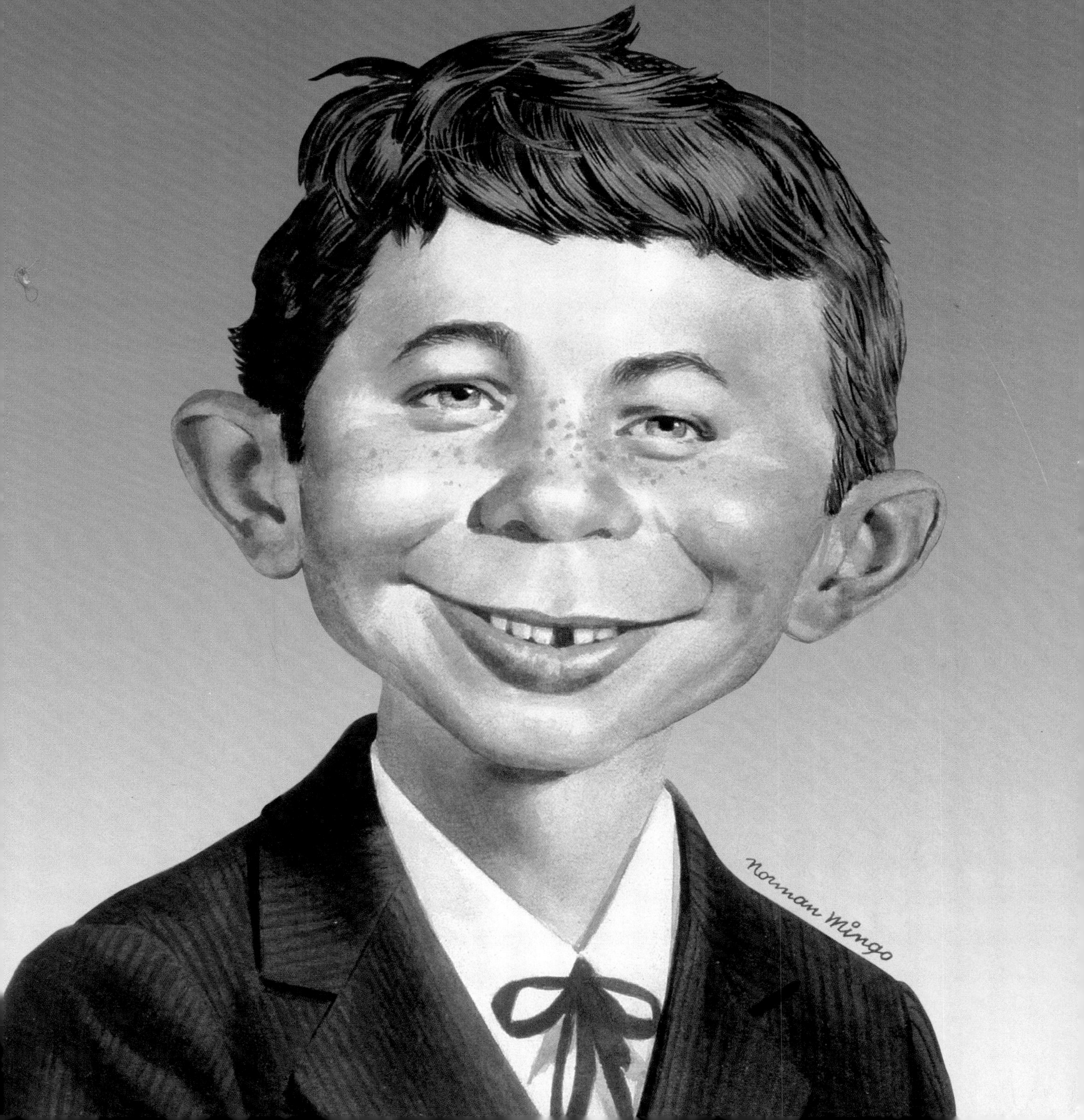
Norman Mingo

NEVER JUDGE A BOOK BY ITS COVER—
with the exception of this one.

The cover of this book is a Photomosaic by Robert Silvers. It is made up of images from the first four hundred *MAD* covers, which together comprise the mind-boggling visage of *MAD*'s idiot cover boy, Alfred E. Neuman.

Since its creation in 1952, *MAD* Magazine has been a cultural touchstone, a barometer of the times. And nowhere is this more evident than on its covers. This is why more importance is placed on the cover than on any other aspect of the magazine.

Twelve times a year, *MAD*'s editorial staff gathers for a cover conference, the purpose of which is to decide who or what will adorn the next issue. The conference can last anywhere from five minutes to five days.

In the search for the Perfect Cover, there are no set rules. Suggestions are made. Positions are taken, then reversed. "We become preoccupied with an eight-hundred-pound gorilla," says co-editor John Ficarra. Sketches are created (usually thumbnailed first by co-editor Nick Meglin and then fleshed out graphically by art director Sam Viviano), old sketches are thrown out and new ones are drawn up, improved, revised, dissected, analyzed, ridiculed, flopped, cut and pasted, laughed at, and eventually, approved.

In the end, the gorilla is caged and the staff can return to the task of filling the forty-eight pages *inside* the magazine.

Publisher Bill Gaines

Editor Harvey Kurtzman

Presented here are the first 400 covers, starting with the 23 issues of the comic book *MAD* and continuing through to the present with 377 issues of *MAD* the magazine.

The covers of the comic book *MAD*, like the material within, were the one-man domain of writer/artist/editor Harvey Kurtzman. He alone determined the content and graphic end product, leaving little to chance. Of the first ten covers, he devised all the cover gags and illustrated eight of them himself.

Starting with *MAD* #11 Kurtzman discarded the original format and design he created and devised a series of even more groundbreaking covers unique in the comic book world. On newsstands each one stood out among the dozens of other comics and magazines being produced.

But after a few years Kurtzman was restless in comics and was looking for new challenges. He felt he had taken the early *MAD* as far as it could go and was experiencing feelings of burnout. Also, he had been entertaining a job offer from *Pageant,* a successful "slick" magazine, and was thinking of leaving.

Not wanting to lose Kurtzman, EC Comics publisher, Bill Gaines, made an offer he was certain his editor could not refuse:

"Harvey, you once told me you wanted to turn *MAD* into a slick. Stay, and I'll let you do it."

Editor Al Feldstein (top) and art director John Putnam (bottom)

Kurtzman agreed and Gaines felt relieved. Because of pressures from a Senate subcommittee hearing to investigate the causes of juvenile delinquency, combined with the repressive, newly formed Comics Code, Gaines had been forced to abandon his horror and crime titles. By transforming *MAD* into a twenty-five-cent (cheap!) black-and-white magazine, and to keep Kurtzman in the fold, *MAD* would not be bound (and gagged) by the restrictions of the Code.

MAD the magazine premiered in July 1955 and was an astonishing success. The first issue (#24) instantly sold out and had to be reprinted—a feat unheard of in magazine publishing.

Kurtzman's covers for the new *MAD* were oddball attention-grabbers, similar in tone to those of the comic book. He edited five issues and then, after a power struggle with Gaines, departed to edit *Trump* for *Playboy* publisher Hugh Hefner. (Unfortunately for Kurtzman, *Trump* lasted only two issues.)

MAD's new editor, Al Feldstein, was not essentially a humor writer, and favored a more balanced approach to satire, feeling that there had been too much of one kind—Kurtzman's. "I thought there were signs of *MAD* going off on a tangent, and I tried to stop it," Feldstein said years later.

The new regime's first major innovation was to give the magazine a persona. The name Alfred E. Neuman, like many other "nonsense" monikers, had been floating around the EC office for years. So had the face of the gap-toothed "What—Me Worry?" idiot kid. Feldstein and his staff—associate editors Nick Meglin and Jerry DeFuccio, and art directors John Putnam and Len Brenner—paired the name and the grinning face and made Alfred E. Neuman *MAD*'s symbol. It proved a masterstroke.

And so it was that the "What—Me Worry?" boy made his debut in the fall of 1956 on the cover of issue #30. Within a year he would become a publishing icon, rivaling the *Playboy* bunny and *Esquire*'s debonair Esky.

The staff found that Alfred could fit in most anywhere—on Mount Rushmore (#31), in a fireworks display (#34), even as a headless horseman (#59). To beef up his celebrity status, he was seated with a host of advertising icons on *MAD*'s 5th Anniversary Issue (#35). Being seen in such company cemented his role as a national figure, proving that an imbecilic nobody could become an imbecilic somebody. Even when a chimpanzee painted a cover (#38), Alfred was present, his face adjoining the *MAD* logo. And always it was Norman Mingo's rendering—the classic Neuman prototype from issue #30—that was referenced, even when another artist was assigned a cover.

Nearly a decade passed, and Alfred had been depicted in so many guises and locales that it became more and more of a challenge to portray him in fresh situations. *MAD*'s movie and TV takeoffs came to the rescue, becoming a fertile breeding ground, with Alfred serving as a cover shill for the satires inside the magazine.

Nonetheless, stardom was slow in coming. Alfred's first gig as an "actor" was on the cover of #86 as Lawrence of Arabia, but he had to wait more than three years before his second role, that of Robin to Adam West's Batman (#105), then nearly two years more until he played Clyde to Faye Dunaway's Bonnie (#119).

From then on, Alfred's show-biz career skyrocketed, his image adorning sixteen movie or TV covers in the next five years. *MAD*'s spoofs of the *Star Trek* and *Star Wars* films always required his presence, further assuring him of continued stardom.

▲ Co-editor Nick Meglin
▶ Co-editor John Ficarra

For the editors it is far easier portraying Alfred in a film satire or sitcom spoof design than it is coming up with nonshow-biz covers. The ideas for these covers—let's call them "generic," for want of a better word—have been generated for the most part by the in-house staff. About 10 percent have been the brainchildren of contributors—i.e., "The Usual Gang of Idiots." Sergio Aragonés leads all outsiders, nosing out Duck Edwing and Al Jaffee. It is probably no coincidence that all three are writer-artists.

Is there a formula for a successful cover? Co-editor Nick Meglin, whose *MAD* career spans some forty years, and who has generated more cover concepts than anyone else associated with the magazine, has his doubts:

"It is a relative process from start to finish. As we approach a deadline, a cover idea, no matter how much we like it, or don't, must be assigned to an artist in

time to make the issue. Some good ideas come out great. Others fail perhaps because the 'mind's eye' has visualized something that in actuality cannot easily be achieved graphically. Sometimes the artist we believe most suitable to a particular design is not available. And sometimes a so-so idea exceeds our expectations because of the skill of the artist.

"We've yet to find a correlation between sales and a well-executed cover. There have been too many times when what we judge as a mediocre execution based on a mediocre idea has resulted in excellent sales, and vice versa. Nonetheless, selecting the cover normally takes precedence over everything else."

For forty years, *MAD*'s covers reflected the overall tone of the magazine—satirical, sometimes slapstick, but rarely controversial—the notable exception being the finger cover (#166), which many retailers refused to display. An unspoken code of expression seemed to exist. There was a line separating the safe from the shocking, and *MAD* preferred not to cross it.

But pop culture was undergoing a sea of change, and co-editors Nick Meglin and John Ficarra, who replaced Al Feldstein in 1984, had to deal with it. In the media all around them, one taboo after another was being shattered and an anything-goes mentality was taking over. *MAD* hesitated. True, the magazine had always treated the world around it with sharp irreverence and mockery, but had drawn the line at blatant bathroom humor and the like.

Eventually, *MAD* was compelled to cross the line. It was a conscious decision, brought about by the country's new morality (or lack of it) and the magazine's shrinking circulation.

The new, "edgier" *MAD* broke wind in April 1997 with Alfred photocopying his butt (#356). Some veteran readers were turned off by the magazine's fresh, "in-your-face" point of view. Younger readers were more comfortable with the changeover. Pairing Howard Stern and Dennis Rodman in a cross-dressing wedding ceremony (#357) would have been unimaginable twenty years earlier. But Stern and Rodman personified the new shock-schlock-jock culture. *MAD,* in tune with the times, could scarcely ignore them.

More telling has been the magazine's view of the presidency. True, Alfred presses his candidacy every four years ("You could do worse and you always have!") but this is a *MAD* tradition and, besides, the idea of an idiot seeking the White House makes as valid a point today as it did in 1956, if not more so.

▲ Art director
Len Brenner

▶ Artist/art director
Sam Viviano

It's been a different story with covers portraying real-life presidents. Consider:

Dwight D. Eisenhower made a single appearance on a *MAD* cover, and a cameo at that (#56). John F. Kennedy (#56, #60, #66) was handled with kid gloves. Lyndon B. Johnson (#56, #114, #122) made group appearances only. Richard Nixon had the dubious distinction of appearing on four covers (#56, #60, #122, #171), but only his last appearance was a zinger (a classic substitution of Nixon and Vice President Agnew as Paul Newman and Robert Redford from 1973's Academy Award winner, *The Sting*). Surprisingly, Gerald Ford was ignored altogether, while Jimmy Carter (#197) was merely a subject of whimsy. Ronald Reagan was seen three times (#122, #255, #259), but only his third appearance dealt with his politics. George Bush made the cover twice (#312, #315), with only the first one making a personal point, albeit a gastric one (his vomiting in Japan).

Then along came Bill Clinton, attaining cover notoriety (#325, #331, #361, #377) during *MAD*'s new edgier era. He was broadsided, especially on the Monopoly cover (#361), which savaged his political and personal life. Probably more than any other, this cover epitomizes the new *MAD*.

The freewheeling America of today seems far removed from that of the straitlaced 1950s. The early *MAD* covers, once considered audacious, appear tame in light of the so-called new freedom. Yet *MAD*'s basic intent has remained constant: Shield no sacred cows; spare neither the right nor left; be conned by no one; take no prisoners. Politics, the media, sports, advertising—all are fair game.

Seen in chronological order, the covers of *MAD* emerge as a kind of pictorial time capsule. Nearly all hit their mark, some spectacularly so, and in the pages that follow, these are singled out. A few land with a thud, and these get their due as well.

Twelve covers receive special attention—the ones honored as the "Soul of *MAD*"—#30, #31, #32, #36, #38, #43, #94, #96, #126, #153, #154, and #171. To the staff they are priceless, the cream of the crop. Each one is framed and displayed in *MAD*'s offices. The editors have vowed that the original art for these will never be sold, no matter how high the offer.

For those left wondering, the last "Soul of *MAD*" cover appeared in 1974. Because of a policy decision to return the original artwork to the artists, *MAD* would have to buy back the covers in order to frame them alongside the others. Notoriously cheap, the magazine would never consider this possibility. Complicating matters further, it would be difficult to determine exactly which of the later covers would make that hallowed list. Probably none, "if only because we haven't had a good cover since then," quips co-editor John Ficarra. You be the judge.

So here they are, together at last—four hundred *MAD* covers spanning nearly half a century. Nothing more needs to be said, so turn the pages and follow the course of *MAD* through the years, from cover to cover.

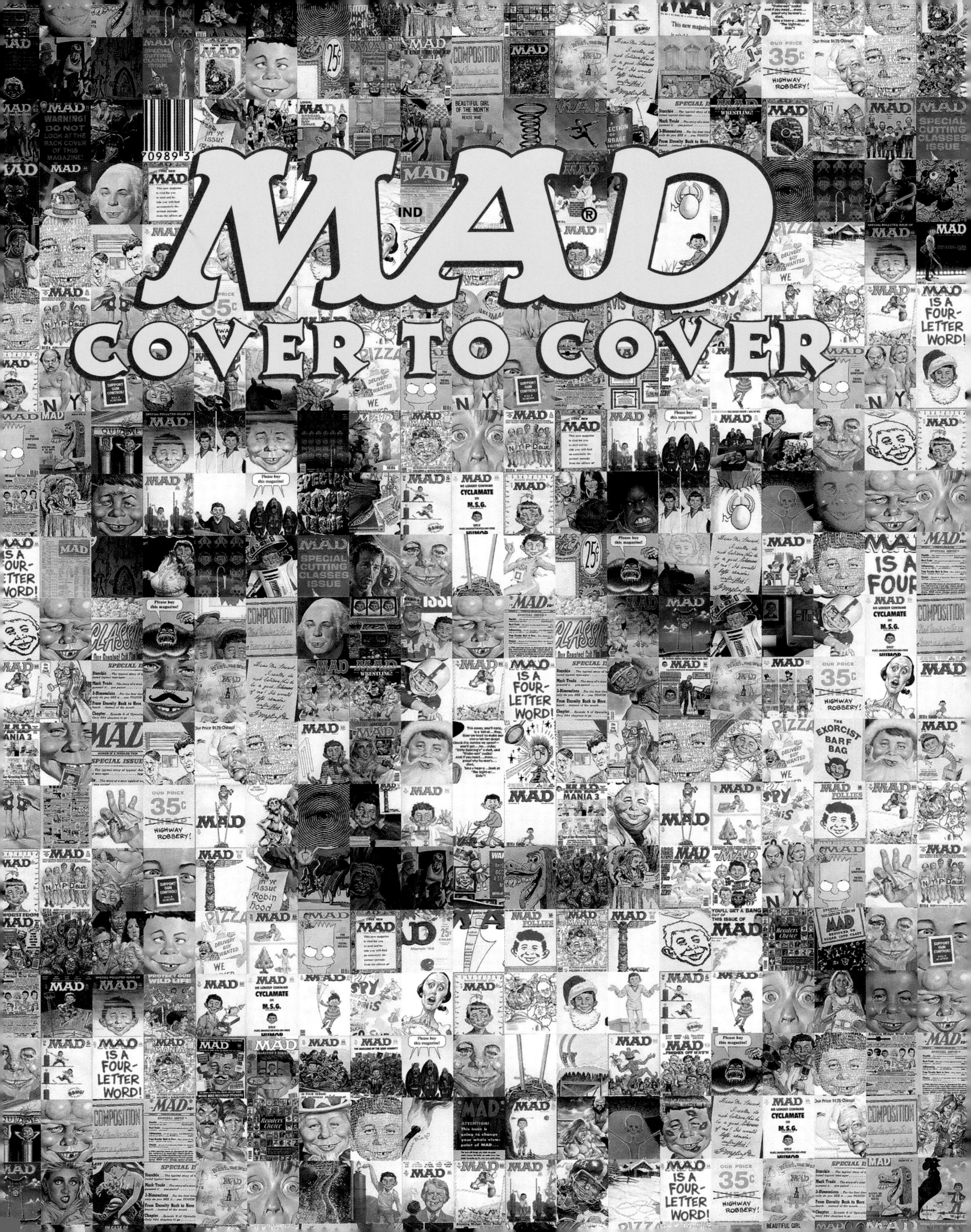
MAD®
COVER TO COVER

MAD #1
October–November 1952
ARTIST: Harvey Kurtzman
WRITER: Harvey Kurtzman

Preliminary cover sketch for *MAD #1*
by Harvey Kurtzman

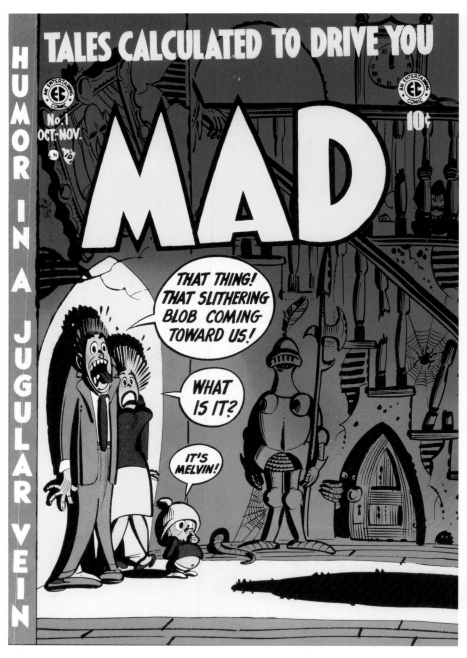

"Greetings, you MAD readers! You're now holding in your MAD hands the very first MAD issue of MAD!" Emblazoned on the inside front cover, this proclamation welcomed readers into the fold. The cover of #1, rendered by editor Harvey Kurtzman, spoofs EC's horror comics—a genre he disliked—and reveals his fondness for the name Melvin. Later issues of the comic book *MAD* would feature "Little Orphan Melvin!" "Melvin of the Apes!" and "Smilin' Melvin!" Moreover, the famed "gap-toothed boy" image introduced by Kurtzman was often referred to in the magazine as Melvin Cowznofski (later to become Alfred E. Neuman).

The original art for this cover was bought by director Steven Spielberg in 1986 for $15,500 (at that time a record price for a comic book cover).

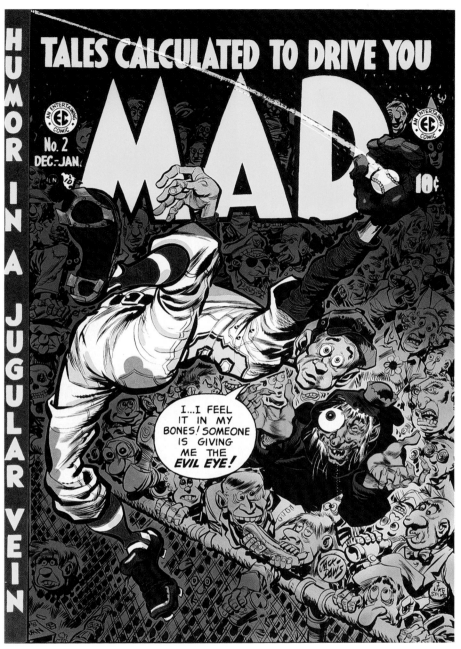

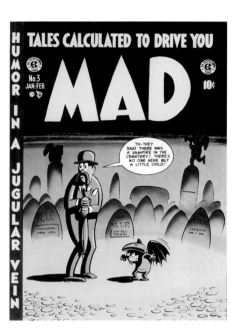

◄ *MAD #2*
December 1952–January 1953
ARTIST: Jack Davis
WRITER: Harvey Kurtzman

▲ *MAD #3*
January–February 1953
ARTIST: Harvey Kurtzman
WRITER: Harvey Kurtzman

Hand colored by Harvey Kurtzman, this "silver print" for *MAD #2* was used as a guide for the printer. Handwriting by Bill Gaines. From the collection of Len Brenner

Artist Jack Davis's only cover for the comic book *MAD,* and one of the few not illustrated by Kurtzman. A rabid sports fan, Davis enjoyed depicting spectacles of athletic mayhem, as evidenced here. When Kurtzman departed from *MAD* in 1956, Davis followed, then returned in 1965 as a *MAD* regular.

Artist Jack Davis. Photo by Irving Schild (October 1993)

▼ **MAD #4**
April–May 1953
ARTIST: Harvey Kurtzman
WRITER: Harvey Kurtzman

▶ **MAD #5**
June–July 1953
ARTIST: Will Elder
WRITER: Harvey Kurtzman

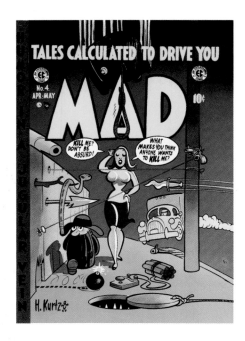

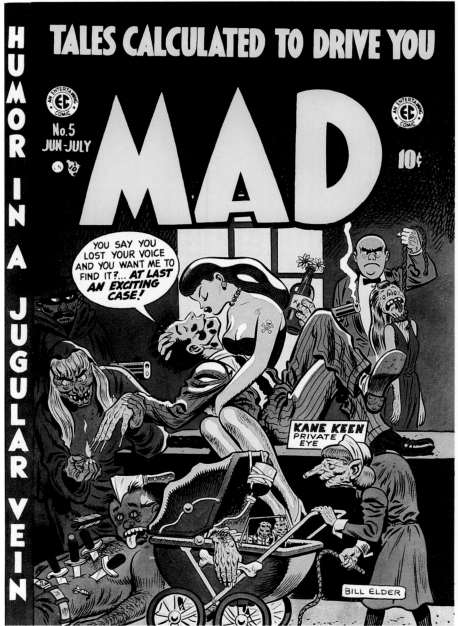

Preliminary cover sketch for *MAD #4* by Harvey Kurtzman. From the collection of Glenn Bray. Reprinted with permission from *Tales of Terror— The EC Companion* by Grant Geissman and Fred von Bernewitz (Gemstone/Fantagraphics, 2000)

Will Elder's sole comic book *MAD* cover reveals his unique brand of lunacy. Elder looked on Kurtzman as a mentor, and the two continued to collaborate throughout their careers, even after they left the magazine together in 1956. He and Kurtzman returned briefly to *MAD* in the mid-1980s, working on several covers (#259, #261, #268) as well as interior articles.

MAD #6
August–September 1953
ARTIST: Harvey Kurtzman
WRITER: Harvey Kurtzman

MAD #7
October–November 1953
ARTIST: Harvey Kurtzman
WRITER: Harvey Kurtzman

▲ Hand colored by Harvey Kurtzman, this "silver print" for *MAD* #6 was used as a guide for the printer. Handwriting by Harvey Kurtzman. From the collection of Len Brenner

▶ Preliminary cover sketch for *MAD* #10 by Harvey Kurtzman. Reprinted with permission from *Collectibly MAD* by Grant Geissman (Kitchen Sink Press, 1995)

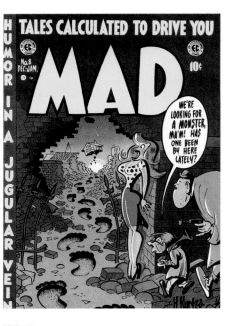

MAD #8
December 1953–January 1954
ARTIST: Harvey Kurtzman
WRITER: Harvey Kurtzman

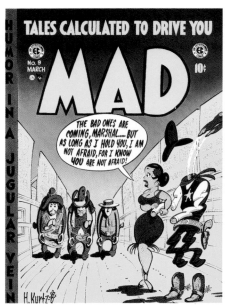

MAD #9
March 1954
ARTIST: Harvey Kurtzman
WRITER: Harvey Kurtzman

MAD #10
April 1954
ARTIST: Harvey Kurtzman
WRITER: Harvey Kurtzman

MAD #11
May 1954

ARTIST: Basil Wolverton
WRITER: Harvey Kurtzman

◄ Artist Basil Wolverton. From the collection of Monte Wolverton

The genesis of this cover predates *MAD* by eight years. In 1946, in his immensely popular comic strip *Li'l Abner*, Al Capp introduced—but did not picture—Lena the Hyena, "the ugliest woman in Lower Slobbovia." What did Lena look like? Newspapers ran local contests and were deluged with entries depicting ugly females, most of which were too repulsive to print. (*MAD*'s Jack Davis, then a college freshman, won the statewide contest in Georgia.)

Capp sponsored a nationwide competition, offering a $500 prize for the best, most appropriately hideous Lena. The winner was Basil Wolverton, whose rendering (below) garnered much publicity, including a spread in *Life* magazine. A self-described "Producer of Preposterous Pictures of Peculiar People Who Prowl This Perplexing Planet," Wolverton has been referred to as "the Rube Goldberg of the human anatomy" and "an adherent of the spaghetti-and-meatball school of design."

Recalling the contest and needing an eye-catching cover for his mock *Life* issue, Kurtzman commissioned Wolverton to create a Lena-like portrait for *MAD* #11. (The background photo is said to have been taken from the men's room window of the *MAD* offices, then located at 225 Lafayette Street in downtown New York.)

Although Wolverton illustrated only a handful of memorable articles for *MAD*, his grotesque faces and images have reappeared in the magazine over the years, even gracing the *MAD* NHRA (National Hot Rod Association) "Ugly Car" in 2000.

Monte Wolverton, Basil's son, carries on the family tradition. His work, which is not unlike that of his father (although more the "linguini-and-clam-sauce school of design"), can be seen in the pages of today's *MAD*.

TALES CALCULATED TO DRIVE YOU...

MAD 10¢

*****This special issue is designed for people ashamed to read this comic-book in subways and like that! Merely hold cover in front of face making sure it's not upside down. MAD cover design makes people think you are reading high-class intellectual stuff instead of miserable junk.**

▲ **MAD #12**
June 1954
WRITER: Harvey Kurtzman

▶ **MAD #13**
July 1954
ARTIST: Harvey Kurtzman
WRITER: Harvey Kurtzman

In retrospect, Kurtzman had mixed feelings about this cover. True, he knocked it out faster than usual, but looking back he called it "a jokeless joke," explaining "I was intrigued by the graphics of the thing, just doing a teeny-weeny thing with empty space, as opposed to the traditional comics that come at you again and again with everything big, big, big." The cover had no effect on newsstand sales, which remained brisk.

Hand colored by Harvey Kurtzman, this "silver print" for *MAD* #13 was used as a guide for the printer. Handwriting by Harvey Kurtzman.
From the collection of Annie Gaines

MAD #14
August 1954
ARTIST: Leonardo da Vinci
WRITER: Harvey Kurtzman

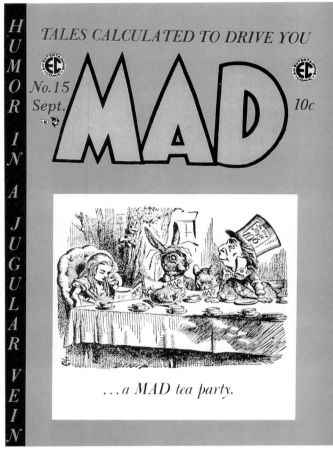

MAD #15
September 1954
ARTIST: Sir John Tenniel
WRITER: Harvey Kurtzman

We can only guess why da Vinci's Mona Lisa is smiling, but she might have been amused to learn that several dozen *MAD* readers mistook her for the Virgin Mary, their irate letters accusing the magazine of being sacrilegious.

The following cover (#15) also appropriated an art icon—Sir John Tenniel's "mad tea party" illustration for Lewis Carroll's *Alice in Wonderland.*

MAD #16
October 1954
ARTIST: Harvey Kurtzman
WRITER: Harvey Kurtzman

MAD #17
November 1954
WRITER: Harvey Kurtzman

LOOK GANG! ANOTHER SURPRISE! IN THIS ISSUE...YOU DRAW THE COVER!

▲ **MAD #18**
December 1954
ARTIST: Harvey Kurtzman
WRITER: Harvey Kurtzman

▶ **MAD #19**
January 1955
WRITER: Harvey Kurtzman

Gags abound in this parody of a racing form. The density of jokes, so identified with the articles inside the magazine, has now made its way onto the cover. Note the results of the third and fourth races at Laurel, which are the first words of "That's Amore," popularized by Dean Martin. Also worthy of mention is the list of entries for the first race at Gulfstream, in which Chicken, Wildcat, Rosebush, Barbed Wire, Mosquito, and Poison Ivy are "scratched." Reading time for the cover may exceed that for the rest of the magazine (and this book as well!).

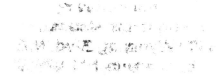

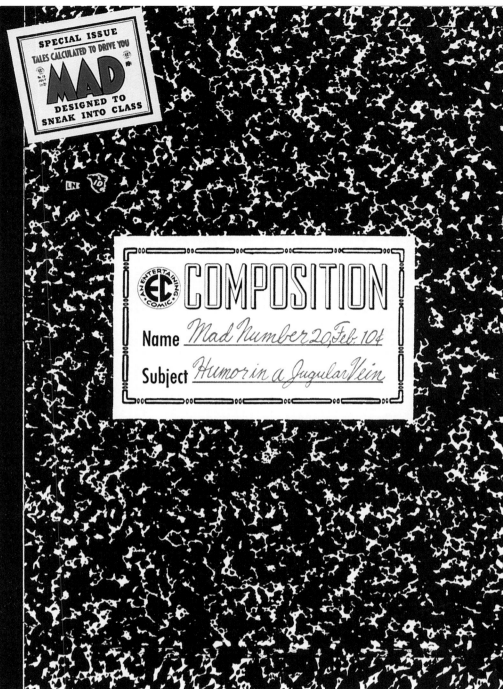

MAD #20
February 1955
WRITER: Harvey Kurtzman

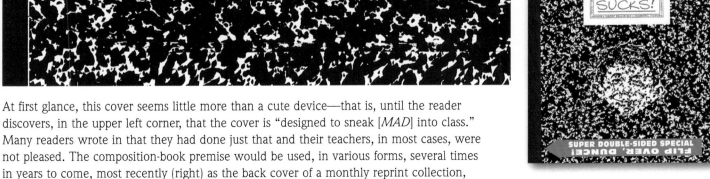

At first glance, this cover seems little more than a cute device—that is, until the reader discovers, in the upper left corner, that the cover is "designed to sneak [*MAD*] into class." Many readers wrote in that they had done just that and their teachers, in most cases, were not pleased. The composition-book premise would be used, in various forms, several times in years to come, most recently (right) as the back cover of a monthly reprint collection, *MAD Super Special* #137 (May 1999).

19

MAD #21

March 1955

WRITER: Harvey Kurtzman

For sheer number of words no cover exceeds this one, a spoof of those multiproduct ads found in many comic books of the era. Offerings include a throwing dagger knife ("Hunt small game and small friends"), a live crocodile ("Great fun!"), and a Gatling gun ("Good for shooting bloody 'eathens"). Look closely and you will find an early version of the character who would come to be known as Alfred E. Neuman.

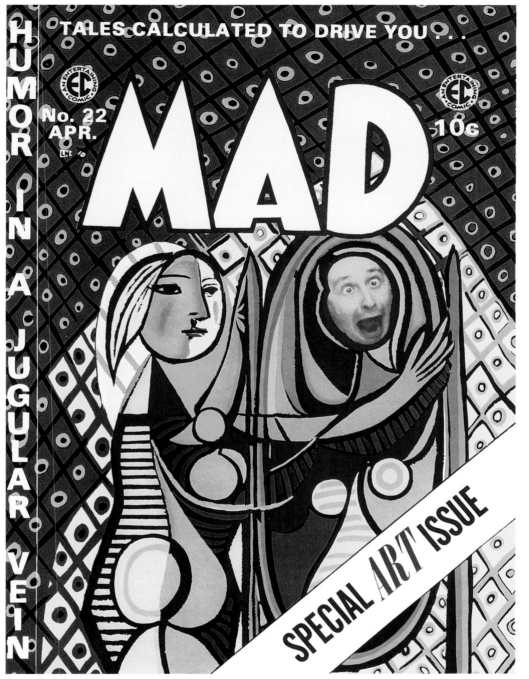

TALES CALCULATED TO DRIVE YOU...

HUMOR IN A JUGULAR VEIN

EC AN ENTERTAINING COMIC

No. 22 APR.

MAD

10¢

SPECIAL ART ISSUE

◀ **MAD #22**

April 1955

ARTIST: Harvey Kurtzman

WRITER: Harvey Kurtzman

TALES CALCULATED TO DRIVE YOU

HUMOR IN A JUGULAR VEIN

No. 23 May

MAD

10¢

THINK

▲ **MAD #23**

May 1955

WRITER: Harvey Kurtzman

The human face in this Picasso-like cover belongs to Will Elder (right) who, along with Jack Davis and Wally Wood, was among the most prolific of the comic book *MAD*'s early artists. The entire issue (illustrated by Elder) was devoted to him as well, chronicling his life from early childhood ("from the time he was a tiny, miserable two-bit hack infant") to "senility."

Artist Will Elder

MAD #24
July 1955
WRITER: Harvey Kurtzman
BORDER ARTISTS: Harvey Kurtzman
and Will Elder
LOGO: Harvey Kurtzman

THE NEW

MAD

NO. 24 ✳ HUMOR IN A JUGULAR VEIN ✳ JULY 1955

This new magazine
is vital for you
to read and in-
side you will find
an extremely im-
portant message
from the editors ☞

25¢

The comic book *MAD* was history. In 1955 it evolved into a "slick"—a twenty-five-cent (cheap!) black-and-white magazine of humor, satire, and parody. The first six covers featured a border. On the lower left corner appears the name Alfred L. Neuman. At the top can be found the face of the "What—Me Worry?" kid, not yet christened Alfred E. Neuman, though the day was soon approaching.

In case you're curious, here's the "extremely important message from the editors" found inside: "Please buy this magazine!"

▲ **MAD #25**
September 1955
ARTIST: Thomas Nast
WRITER: Harvey Kurtzman
BORDER ARTISTS: Harvey Kurtzman and Will Elder
LOGO: Harvey Kurtzman

▼ **MAD #26**
November 1955
ARTIST: Wallace Wood
WRITER: Harvey Kurtzman
BORDER ARTISTS: Harvey Kurtzman and Will Elder
LOGO: Harvey Kurtzman

"*MAD* fearlessly exposes the Tweed Ring," blares the caption. The cover features the enduring political cartoon by Thomas Nast, whose efforts in the 1870s helped bring down the corrupt regime of New York politician William Marcy "Boss" Tweed. What all this had to do with *MAD* #25 is anyone's guess.

▲ **MAD #27**
April 1956
ARTIST: Jack Davis
WRITER: Harvey Kurtzman
BORDER ARTISTS: Harvey Kurtzman and Will Elder
LOGO: Harvey Kurtzman

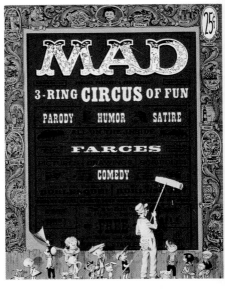

MAD #28
July 1956
ARTIST: Wallace Wood
WRITER: Harvey Kurtzman
BORDER ARTISTS: Harvey Kurtzman and Will Elder

Due to distribution problems, three variations of the cover for *MAD* #28 were produced. From the collection of Michael Lerner

MAD #29
September 1956
ARTIST: Wallace Wood
WRITER: Staff
BORDER ARTISTS: Harvey Kurtzman and Will Elder

▶ **MAD #30**
December 1956
ARTIST: Norman Mingo
WRITER: Staff
BORDER ARTISTS: Harvey Kurtzman
and Will Elder

MAD #30 back cover

The year 1956 marked the start of a new regime, with Al Feldstein taking over as editor after the departure of Harvey Kurtzman. One of the first decisions of the editorial staff was to combine the face of the "idiot kid" with the name Alfred E. Neuman and make him *MAD*'s official mascot and cover boy.

Early versions of Alfred possessed a muddy, archaic look, so Feldstein advertised for a young new cover artist. The man hired was sixty-year-old Norman Mingo, a former magazine illustrator and the only veteran of World War I ever to work for *MAD*. Mingo came out of retirement and took on the task of creating the perfect Alfred. He succeeded, and his rendering became the prototype for all subsequent depictions of Alfred.

MAD #30 portrays Alfred as a presidential candidate, a role he would assume in all future White House elections. Although his name was originally Alfred *L.* Neuman, with this issue *MAD*'s art director John Putnam changed the initial to an "E," which he felt gave the name a certain panache. Years later, it was suggested by associate editor Jerry DeFuccio that the "E" should stand for "Enigma."

This cover is the first of only twelve to be honored in the pantheon called the "Soul of *MAD*."

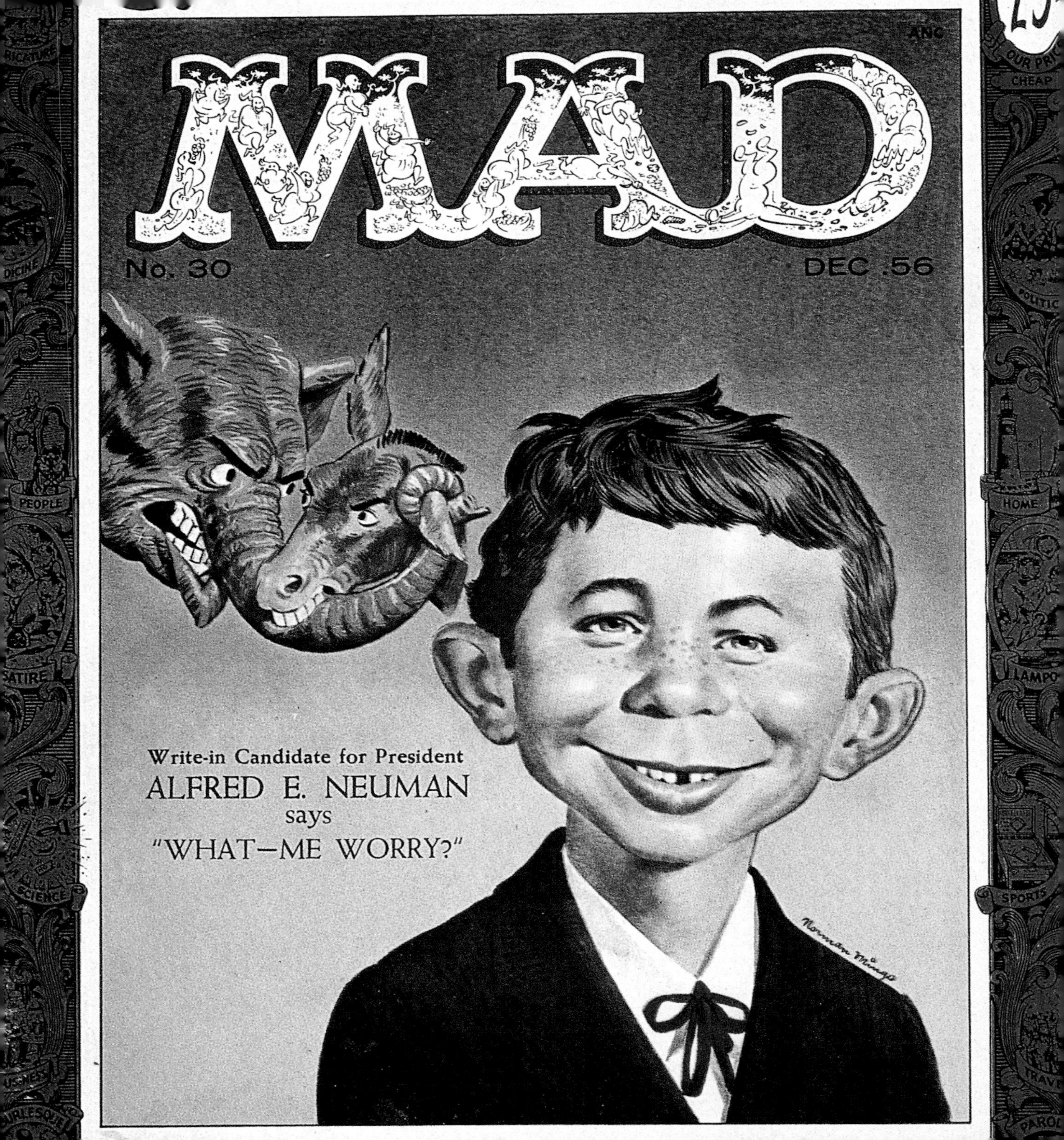
MAD
No. 30
DEC. 56
Write-in Candidate for President
ALFRED E. NEUMAN
says
"WHAT—ME WORRY?"
Norman Mingo
PEOPLE
SATIRE
SCIENCE
BURLESQUE
HOME
SPORTS
CHEAP

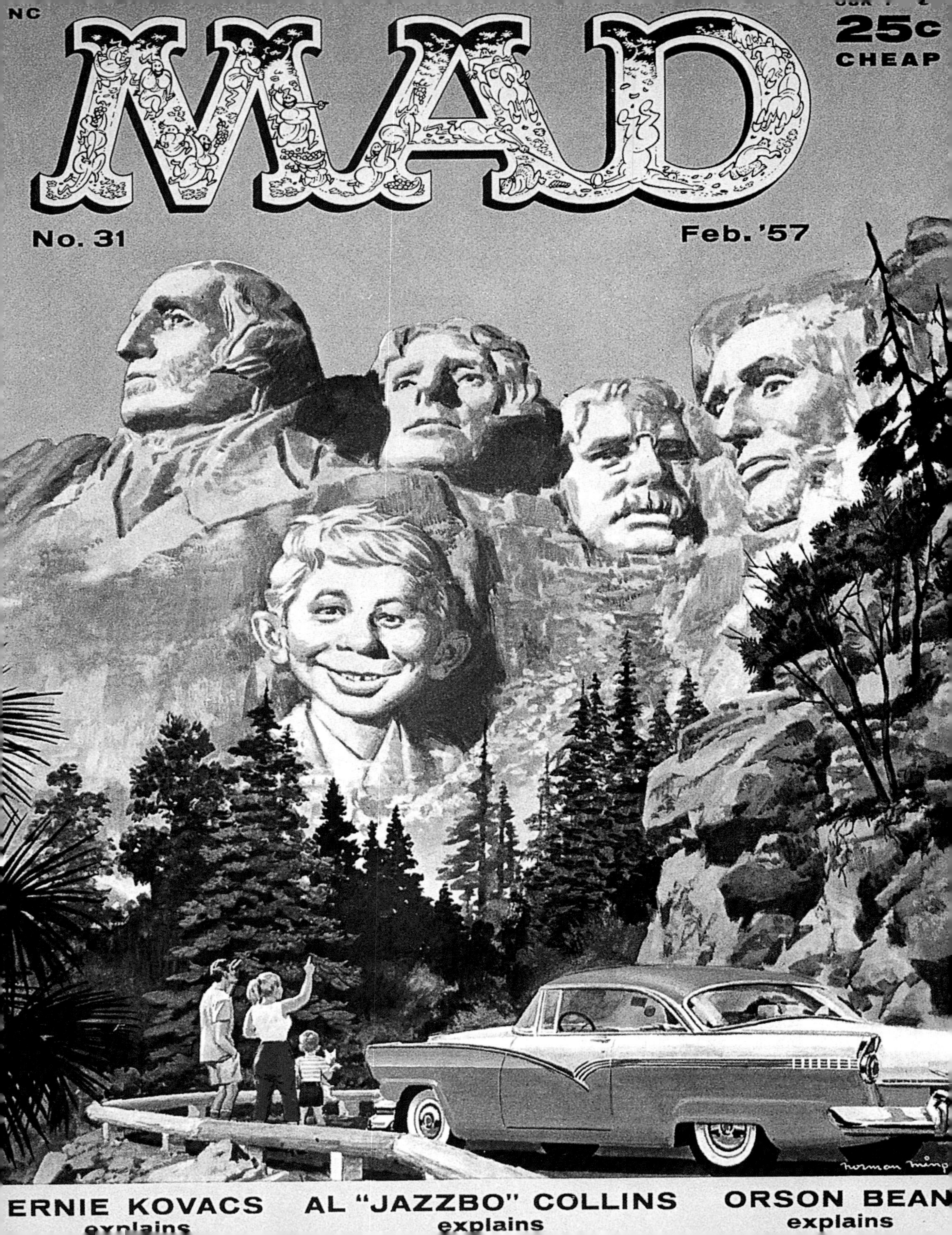
NC
MAD
25c
CHEAP
No. 31
Feb. '57
ERNIE KOVACS
explains
AL "JAZZBO" COLLINS
explains
ORSON BEAN
explains

◄ *MAD #31*
February 1957
ARTIST: Norman Mingo
WRITER: Staff
LOGO: Harvey Kurtzman

Despite Alfred's being elevated to Mount Rushmore status on cover #31, not everyone at *MAD* was instantly sold on the idea of using him as the magazine's continuing cover boy. Nick Meglin, then an assistant editor, thought otherwise. He was challenged by publisher Bill Gaines to come up with at least five cover concepts featuring Alfred. Playing up to Gaines's interest in archeology, Meglin included a rough sketch of Alfred in an Egyptian tomb (#32), and one or two others that emerged as cover concepts later. Having been convinced there were endless cover possibilities, Gaines (thankfully!) agreed that from then on Alfred should reign as the magazine's icon.

Mingo's Mount Rushmore artwork was reused thirty years later by the Quality Paperback Book Club for their cover of the 1997 anthology *MAD About the Fifties* (below left). Later, artist Mark Stutzman would also reprise the image, replacing the four presidents with a quartet of wannabes (Warren Beatty, Patrick Buchanan, Jesse Ventura, and Donald Trump). Titled "A Monumental Disaster," it served as the back cover for issue #389 (below right).

Both #31 and #32 are "Soul of *MAD*" covers.

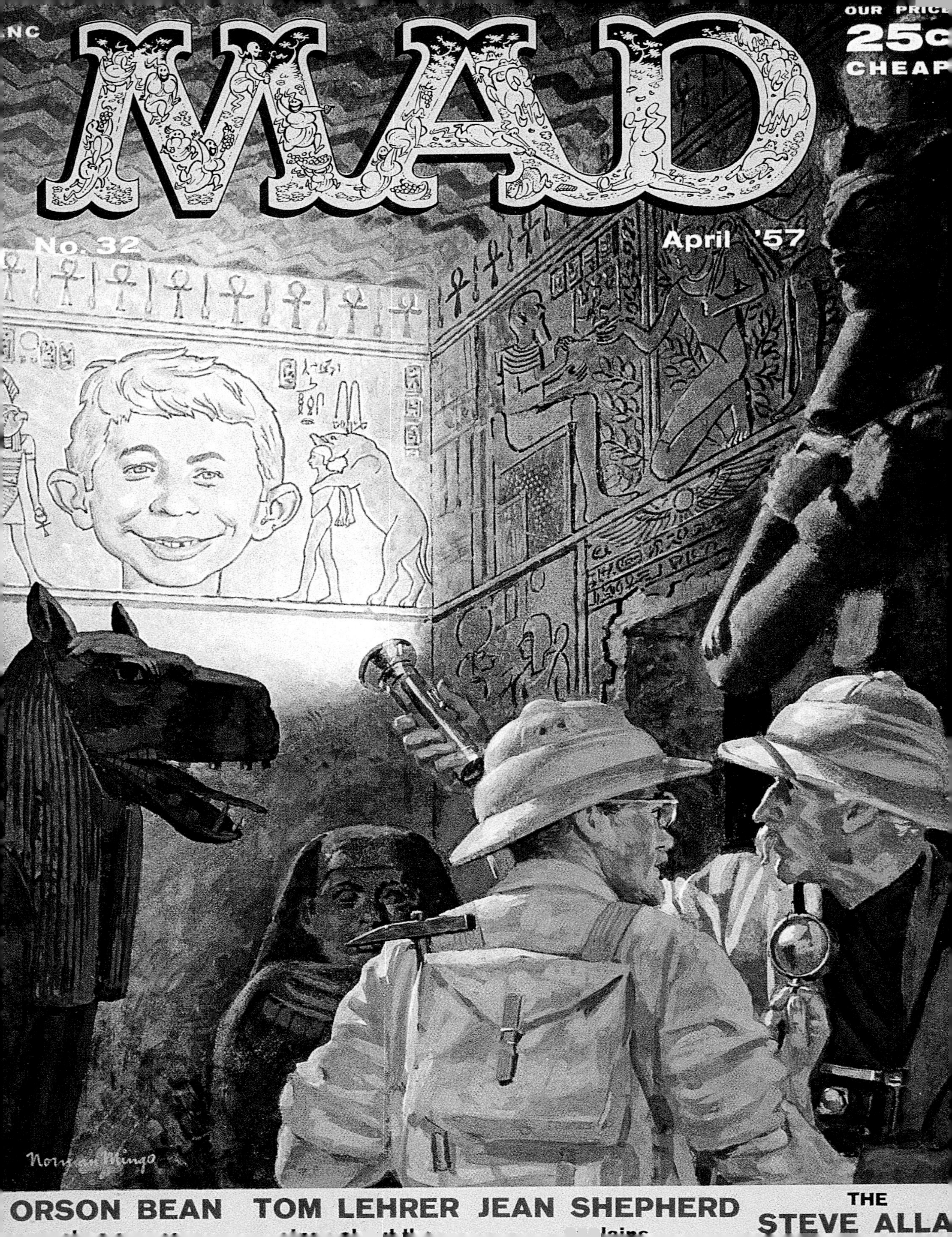

OUR PRIC
25c
CHEAP
MAD
No. 32
April '57
Norman Mingo
ORSON BEAN
TOM LEHRER
JEAN SHEPHERD
THE
STEVE ALLA

MAD #33
June 1957
ARTIST: Norman Mingo
WRITER: Staff
LOGO: Harvey Kurtzman

ERNIE KOVACS
"Strangely Believe It"
HENRY MORGAN
"The Truth About Cowboys"
THE OLD PHILOSOPHER
EDDIE LAWRENCE
"The Disc Jockey's Lament"
Hollywood is Ruining
MARLIN BRANDO

MAD #34
August 1957
ARTIST: Norman Mingo
WRITER: Staff
LOGO: Harvey Kurtzman

▼ **MAD #35**
October 1957
ARTIST: Norman Mingo
WRITER: Staff
LOGO: Harvey Kurtzman

◄ **MAD #32**
April 1957
ARTIST: Norman Mingo
WRITER: Staff
LOGO: Harvey Kurtzman

Norman Mingo's experience as an advertising illustrator served him well in rendering *MAD*'s first wraparound cover (above). Fast becoming a national icon, Alfred shared the magazine's fifth anniversary celebration with a host of merchandising characters. Among them: Betty Crocker, Uncle Ben, the Campbell's Soup kids, and the Jolly Green Giant.

Although *MAD* would usually treat advertising and its various symbols as targets of ridicule, was this one of those rare times they were treated with respect? Not a chance. By picturing them alongside Alfred, they were clearly being dragged down to his level.

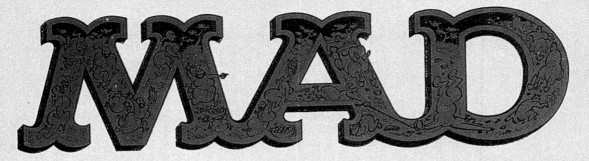

MAD

OUR PRICE
25c
CHEAP

IND

No. 36   Dec. '57

Norman Mingo

WALLY COX

BOB & RAY

◄ **MAD #36**
December 1957
ARTIST: Norman Mingo
WRITER: Staff
LOGO: Harvey Kurtzman

A cover gag so remarkable for its simplicity that any caption would have watered down its impact. Often overlooked is the apple being systematically consumed.

The cover is the fourth honored as the "Soul of *MAD.*"

MAD #37
January 1958
ARTIST: Norman Mingo
WRITER: Staff
LOGO: Harvey Kurtzman

Alfred ushers in 1958. Forty-one years later, this artwork would serve as the cover for a *MAD* Super Special (#141), commenting on Y2K (below).

SPECIAL ISSUE: A CHIMPANZEE
PAINTED THIS COVER OF...

OUR PRICE
25c
CHEAP

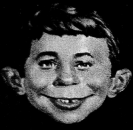

WHAT, ME WORRY?

No. 38

March '58

COVER ARTIST

◄ *MAD #38*
March 1958
ARTIST: J. Fred Muggs
WRITER: Staff
LOGO: Harvey Kurtzman

Alfred takes second billing to J. Fred Muggs, a chimpanzee featured on the *Today Show*, hosted by Dave Garroway. *MAD* commissioned the chimp to finger-paint the cover for an undisclosed fee. In the course of painting, Muggs proved a temperamental artist and bit editor Al Feldstein. Needless to say, the chimp was given no further assignments for the magazine.

This cover was a personal favorite of Bill Gaines. At his insistence (and after he bit the fingers of editors Meglin and Ficarra to prove his point), it became the fifth "Soul of *MAD*" honoree.

► *MAD #39*
May 1958
ARTIST: C. C. Beall Jr.
WRITER: Staff
LOGO: Harvey Kurtzman

...fred is composed of twenty-odd ...miliar images, including Elvis, Lucy ...d Desi, Jerry Lewis, even a '58 Chevy ...l fin. The cover was the work of ...atercolorist C. C. Beall Jr., who had ...eviously painted similar "find the ...tables" illustrations for other ...spectable" magazines.

...Forty years later, this classic would ...come the inspiration for Roberto ...ada's cover for issue #377, the debut ...'The *MAD* 20"—The Dumbest ...ople, Events & Things of 1998.

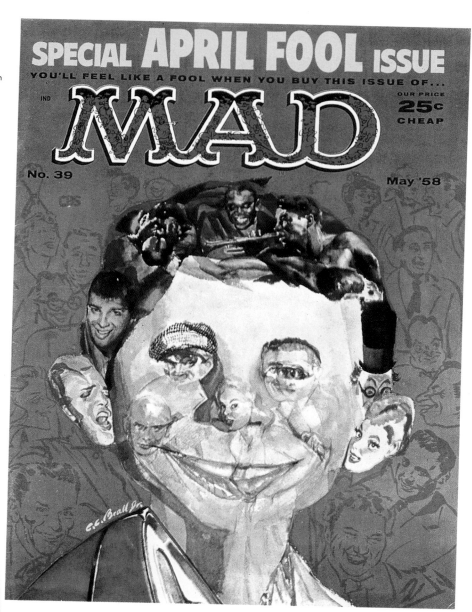

THINK YOU SEE THE FACE OF ALFRED E. NEUMAN, MAD'S ...ATED "WHAT — ME WORRY?" KID, ON OUR FRONT COVER, THEN

PRIL FOOL!

ACTUALLY, ALL YOU'RE SEEING ARE THESE LESSER-KNOWN CHARACTERS:

...rry Piel, (2) Bert Piel, (3) Judy Garland, (4) Bing Crosby, (5) George Gobel, (6) Louis Armstrong, ...oyd Patterson, (8) Number 1 Contender, (9) George Burns, (10) Gracie Allen, (11) Imogene Coca, ...id Caesar, (13) Bob Hope, (14) Ed Wynn, (15) Steve Allen, (16) Ed Sullivan, (17) Jackie Gleason, ...Jerry Lewis, (19) Dave Garroway, (20) Elvis Presley, (21) Rosemary Clooney, (22) Jose Ferrer, (23) ...e Ball, (24) Desi Arnaz, (25) Liberace, (26) Jayne Mansfield, (27) Yul Brynner, (38) Frank Sinatra, (29) Irving Tail-fin.

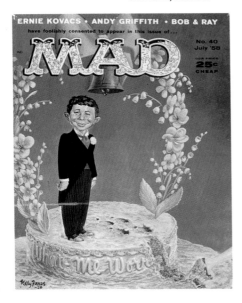

MAD #40
July 1958
ARTIST: Kelly Freas
WRITER: Staff
LOGO: Harvey Kurtzman

DANNY KAYE • ERNIE KOVACS • BOB & RAY

MAD

No. 42

OUR PRICE
25¢
CHEAP

November '58

◄ **MAD #41**
September 1958
ARTIST: Kelly Freas
WRITER: Steve Tuttle
LOGO: Harvey Kurtzman

▲ **MAD #42**
November 1958
ARTIST: Kelly Freas
WRITER: Staff
LOGO: Harvey Kurtzman

► **MAD #43**
December 1958
ARTIST: Kelly Freas
WRITER: Joe Orlando
LOGO: Harvey Kurtzman

How many living things are on this cover? More than fifty, not counting Alfred, whose designation as a living thing is open to question. Of the thirty covers done for the magazine by artist Kelly Freas, this is his personal favorite.

This is the sixth "Soul of *MAD*" cover.

Artist Kelly Freas. Photo courtesy
of Laura Freas

THE SOUL MAD

34

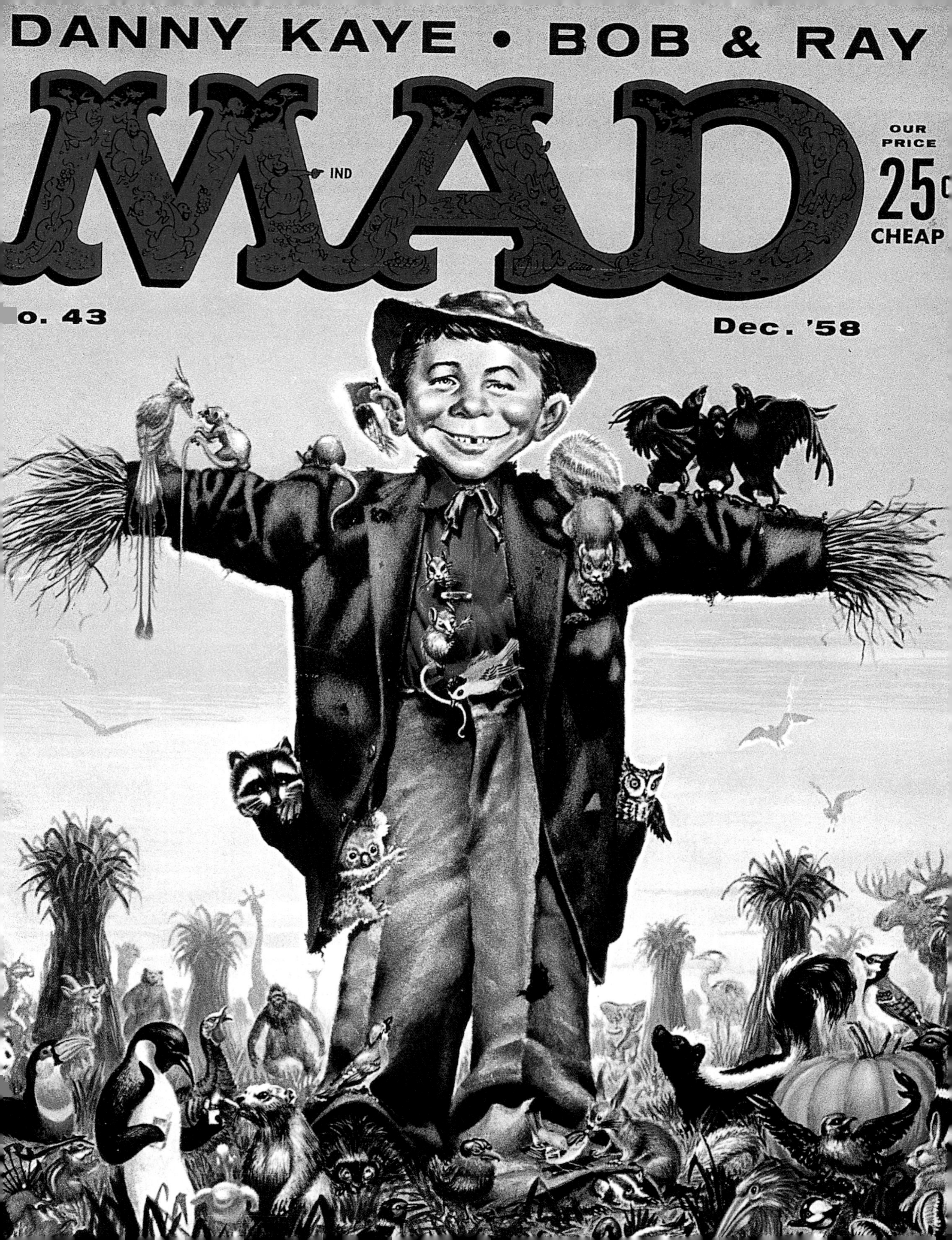
DANNY KAYE • BOB & RAY
MAD
IND
OUR PRICE
25¢
CHEAP
o. 43
Dec. '58

MAD

No. 44

OUR PRICE
25¢
CHEAP

Jan. '59

KELLY FREAS

MAD #44 back cover
ARTIST: Kelly Freas

Did Alfred have a girlfriend? Could a gap-toothed, big-eared, grinning idiot even attract a girlfriend? *MAD*'s editors gave him one, deciding everybody gets lucky once in a while. The lady is Moxie Cowznofski, who debuted on the back cover of #44 (left).

▲ *MAD* #44
January 1959
ARTIST: Kelly Freas
WRITER: Staff
LOGO: Harvey Kurtzman

▶ *MAD* #45
March 1959
ARTIST: Kelly Freas
WRITER: Staff
LOGO: Harvey Kurtzman

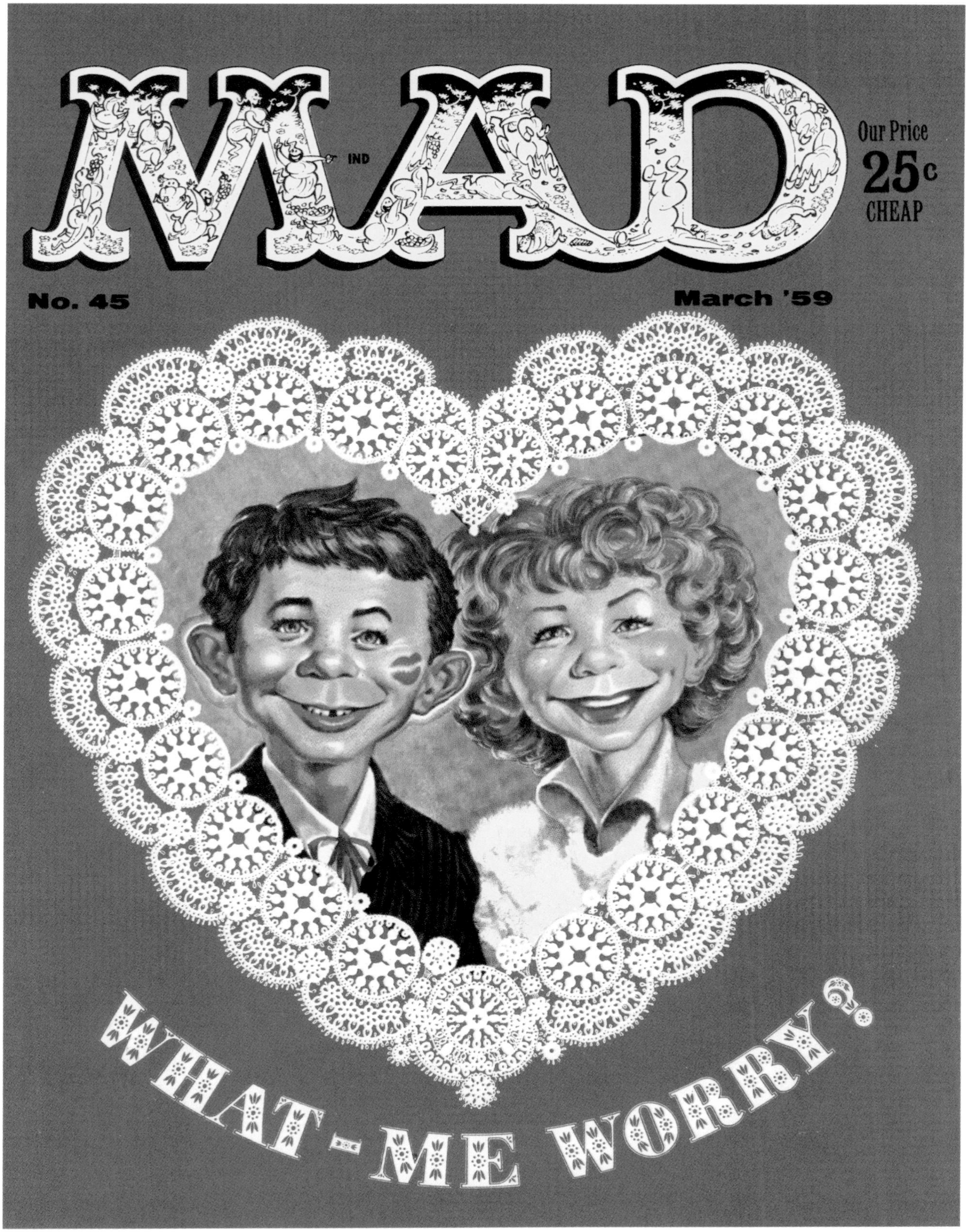
MAD
IND
Our Price
25c
CHEAP
No. 45
March '59
WHAT-ME WORRY?

MAD #46
April 1959
ARTIST: Kelly Freas
WRITER: Staff
LOGO: Harvey Kurtzman

"This cover got a lot of publicity," recalls then–assistant art director Len Brenner. "But who cares?!" Apparently historians do (and hopefully readers).

This issue was a departure, with the rest of the magazine appearing upside down—April Fool! Not surprisingly, some readers believed #46 *was* the final issue. (No such luck!)

MAD #47
June 1959
ARTIST: Kelly Freas
WRITER: Frank Jacobs
LOGO: Harvey Kurtzman

A first for Alfred: We don't see his face, but we do see the back of his head, albeit in the distance. Few readers realize that Alfred is never, but never, shown in profile. This has squelched any thought of his appearing, say, on an FBI front-and-side-view "Wanted" poster. Then again, who would want him?

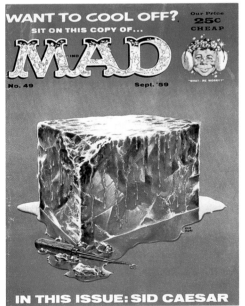

▲ **MAD #48**
July 1959
ARTIST: Kelly Freas
WRITER: Staff
LOGO: Harvey Kurtzman

◄ **MAD #49**
September 1959
ARTIST: Kelly Freas
WRITER: Staff
LOGO: Harvey Kurtzman

MAD #50
October 1959
ARTIST: Kelly Freas
WRITER: Staff
LOGO: Harvey Kurtzman

MAD #51
December 1959
ARTIST: Kelly Freas
WRITER: Staff
LOGO: Harvey Kurtzman

MAD #52
January 1960
ARTIST: Kelly Freas
WRITER: Staff
LOGO: Harvey Kurtzman

MAD #53
March 1960
ARTIST: Kelly Freas
WRITER: Staff
LOGO: Harvey Kurtzman

MAD #54
April 1960
ARTIST: Kelly Freas
WRITER: Staff
LOGO: Harvey Kurtzman

MAD #55
June 1960
ARTIST: Kelly Freas
WRITER: Staff
LOGO: Kelly Freas

MAD #56
July 1960
ARTIST: Kelly Freas
WRITER: Staff
LOGO: Harvey Kurtzman

Election Year 1960—*MAD*'s first cover portraying real-life politicians. Front row (from left): Richard Nixon, John F. Kennedy, Adlai Stevenson, Lyndon B. Johnson. Second row: G. Mennen Williams, Hubert Humphrey, Harry Truman, Stuart Symington, Nelson Rockefeller, Dwight D. Eisenhower. In the background: artist Kelly Freas (with glasses and mustache, behind Truman), Edmund "Pat" Brown (behind Symington), and Edmund Muskie and Estes Kefauver (both behind Rockefeller).

Nixon appeared on four *MAD* covers. He held the record for most presidential appearances for nearly forty years until 1999, when he was tied by Bill Clinton.

◀ *MAD* #58
October 1960
ARTIST: Kelly Freas
WRITER: Dave Berg
LOGO: Harvey Kurtzman

▲ *MAD* #59
December 1960
ARTIST: Kelly Freas
WRITER: Staff
LOGO: Harvey Kurtzman

MAD #60
January 1961
ARTIST: Bob Clarke
WRITER: Staff
LOGO: Harvey Kurtzman

Because this issue was printed six weeks before Election Day 1960, *MAD* took no chances, congratulating both Richard Nixon and John F. Kennedy on the front and back covers. Whatever the outcome, newsstands could feature the winner. As a result *MAD* became the first national magazine to feature President John F. Kennedy on its cover.

In addition to printing two "front covers," the inside of the issue was divided in half and printed right side up/upside down as well—ensuring that no matter which "cover" you opened, you could still read the magazine (well, half of it, anyway).

MAD #61
March 1961
ARTIST: Norman Mingo
WRITER: Staff
LOGO: Harvey Kurtzman

NO MATTER HOW YOU LOOK AT IT—
IT'S GONNA BE A MAD YEAR

No. 61
MARCH '61

OUR PRICE 25c CHEAP

THE LAST UPSIDE-DOWN YEAR UNTIL 6009

1961

THE FIRST UPSIDE-DOWN YEAR SINCE 1881

MAD ushers in 1961, the first upside-down year since 1881, and the last until 6009. By an amazing coincidence, this was also issue #61. In case you're waiting, the cover conference for #6009 isn't scheduled for some time yet.

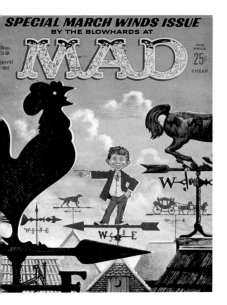

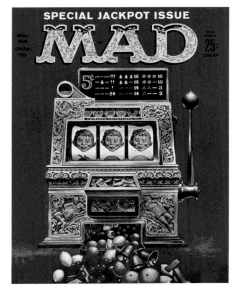

MAD #62

April 1961

ARTIST: Kelly Freas

WRITER: Staff

LOGO: Harvey Kurtzman

MAD #63

June 1961

ARTIST: Kelly Freas

WRITER: Staff

LOGO: Harvey Kurtzman

MAD #64

July 1961

ARTIST: Kelly Freas

WRITER: Staff

LOGO: Harvey Kurtzman

MAD #65

September 1961

ARTIST: Kelly Freas

WRITER: Ilia Rubini

LOGO: Harvey Kurtzman

MAD #66

October 1961

ARTIST: Kelly Freas

WRITER: Staff

LOGO: Harvey Kurtzman

MAD #67

December 1961

ARTIST: Kelly Freas

WRITER: Staff

LOGO: Harvey Kurtzman

MAD #68

January 1962

ARTIST: Don Martin

WRITER: Staff

LOGO: Harvey Kurtzman

The first cover illustrated by "*MAD*'s Maddest Artist," Don Martin, based on an idea by Nick Meglin. Cartoons about rival Santas had been published many times in various periodicals. Martin's no-holds-barred rendering revitalized the premise.

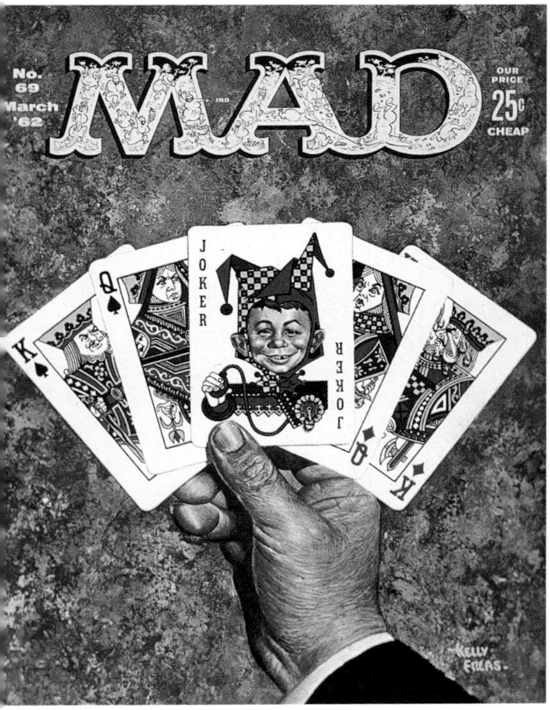
No. 69 March '62
MAD
OUR PRICE 25¢ CHEAP
JOKER
KELLY FREAS

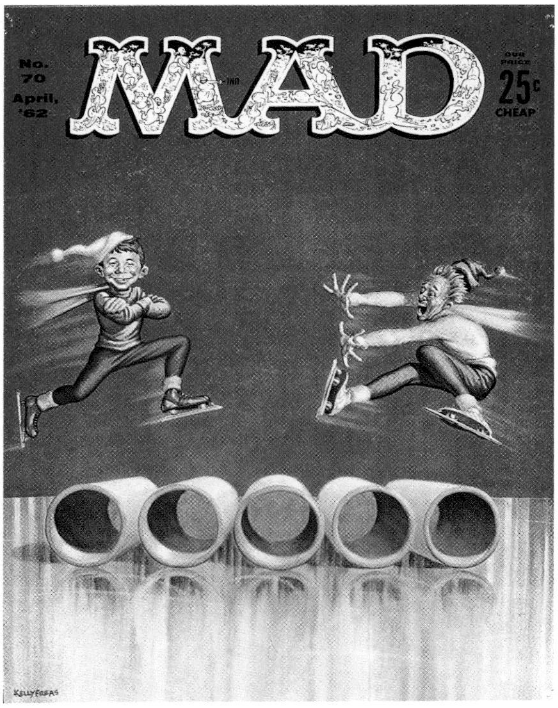
No. 70 April, '62
MAD
OUR PRICE 25¢ CHEAP

◀◀ ***MAD* #69**
March 1962
ARTIST: Kelly Freas
WRITER: Staff
LOGO: Harvey Kurtzman

◀ ***MAD* #70**
April 1962
ARTIST: Kelly Freas
WRITER: Staff
LOGO: Harvey Kurtzman

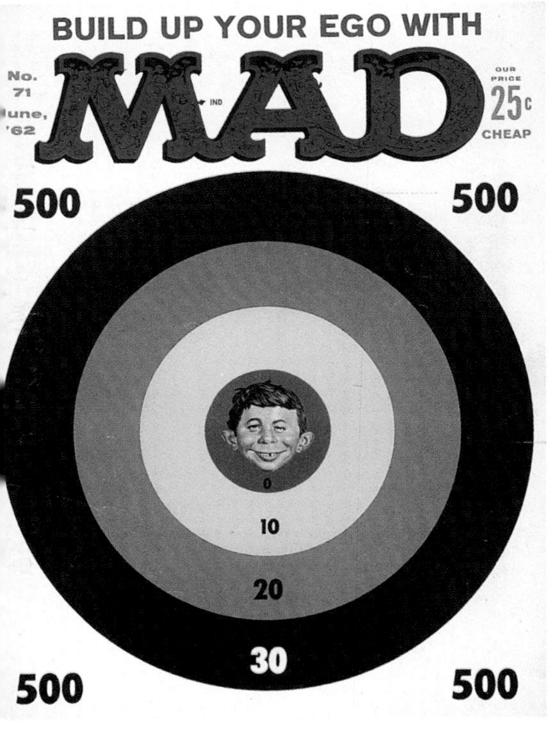
BUILD UP YOUR EGO WITH
No. 71 une, '62
MAD
OUR PRICE 25¢ CHEAP
500
500
0
10
20
30
500
500

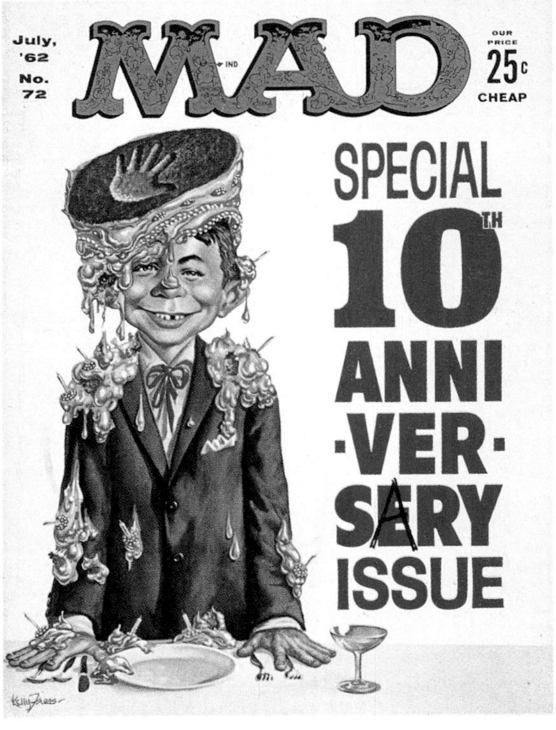
July, '62 No. 72
MAD
OUR PRICE 25¢ CHEAP
SPECIAL
10TH
ANNI
-VER-
SERY
ISSUE

◀◀ ***MAD* #71**
June 1962
ARTIST: Norman Mingo
WRITER: Staff
LOGO: Harvey Kurtzman

◀ ***MAD* #72**
July 1962
ARTIST: Kelly Freas
WRITER: Staff
LOGO: Harvey Kurtzman

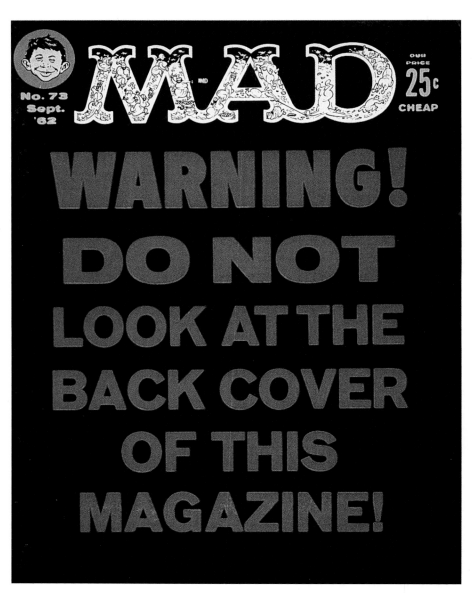

◀ **MAD #73**
September 1962
WRITER: Staff
LOGO: Harvey Kurtzman

▼ **MAD #73 back cover**
ARTIST: Bob Clarke

The Alfred E. Neuman "HEX" Sign

Once you look at it—if you do not buy it for your own—
YOU DIE!
(WELL, WE WARNED YOU NOT TO LOOK!)

The first all-type cover since #24. As a change of pace, *MAD* would concoct pictureless covers every so often. They sold as well as their illustrated brethren (and the art department got to go knock off early for the day!). This convinced the editors that readers were buying the magazine for the *MAD* sensibility and not necessarily for the cover art. Subsequent all-type issues followed with the same success.

▲ **MAD #74**
October 1962
ARTIST: Kelly Freas
WRITER: Staff
LOGO: Harvey Kurtzman

MAD #75
ecember 1962
RTIST: Norman Mingo
RITER: Staff
GO: Harvey Kurtzman

▶ **MAD #76**
January 1963
ARTIST: Norman Mingo
WRITER: Sergio Aragonés
LOGO: Norman Mingo

On a summer's day in 1962, artist Sergio Aragonés walked into the *MAD* offices. An hour later he walked out several hundred dollars richer, having sold the editors the gag for this, his first cover idea of many.

Artist/writer Sergio Aragonés and friend.
MAD relaunch press conference (April 1, 1997)

▼ *MAD* #77
March 1963
ARTIST: Norman Mingo
WRITER: Sergio Aragonés
LOGO: Harvey Kurtzman

◄ *MAD* #78
April 1963
ARTIST: Norman Mingo
WRITER: Sergio Aragonés

▲ *MAD* #79
June 1963
ARTIST: Norman Mingo
WRITER: Staff
LOGO: Harvey Kurtzman

Preliminary cover sketch for
MAD #79 by Norman Mingo.
From the collection of
Richard Landivar

MAD #80
July 1963
ARTIST: Norman Mingo
WRITER: Sergio Aragonés
LOGO: Harvey Kurtzman

e first sequential cover gag. We include this piece of trivia solely to satisfy the
hard *MAD* cultist, whose life would otherwise be incomplete and meaningless.

BUY

MAD

No. 81   Sept. '63

...AND HAVE A BALL!

YOU'LL GET A BANG
OUT OF
THIS ISSUE OF

MAD

October '63
No. 82

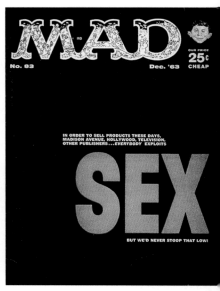
MAD
No. 83   Dec. '63

IN ORDER TO SELL PRODUCTS THESE DAYS,
MADISON AVENUE, HOLLYWOOD, TELEVISION,
OTHER PUBLISHERS...EVERYBODY EXPLOITS

SEX

BUT WE'D NEVER STOOP THAT LOW!

MAD #81

September 1963

ARTIST: Bob Clarke

WRITER: Staff

LOGO: Harvey Kurtzman

MAD #82

October 1963

ARTIST: Norman Mingo

WRITER: Al Jaffee

LOGO: Harvey Kurtzman

MAD #83

December 1963

WRITER: Staff

LOGO: Harvey Kurtzman

SPECIAL CHRISTMAS SEAL ISSUE

MAD

No. 84
Jan. '64

No. 85
March
'64
MAD

MAD #84

January 1964

ARTIST: Norman Mingo

WRITER: Staff

LOGO: Harvey Kurtzman

MAD #85

March 1964

ARTIST: Norman Mingo

WRITER: Staff

LOGO: Harvey Kurtzman

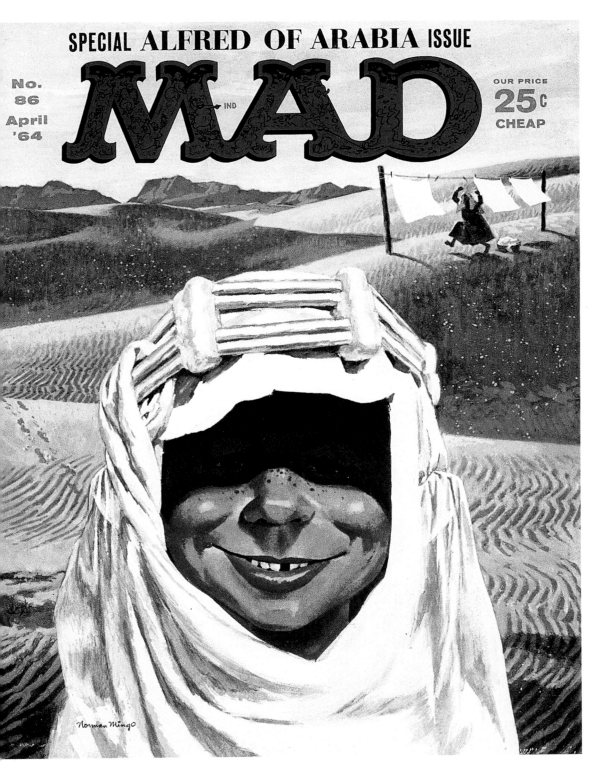

MAD #86
April 1964
ARTIST: Norman Mingo
WRITER: Staff
LOGO: Harvey Kurtzman

Alfred as Lawrence of Arabia—a landmark cover, being the first to promote a movie satire.
Over the years, Alfred has hyped more than one hundred movie and TV spoofs.

▼ *MAD* #87
June 1964
ARTIST: Norman Mingo
WRITER: Staff

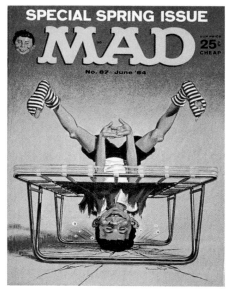

▲ *MAD* #88
July 1964
ARTIST: Norman Mingo
WRITER: Sergio Aragonés

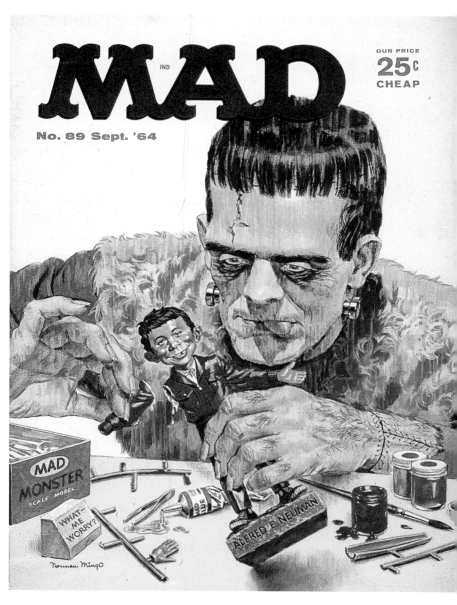

No. 89 Sept. '64

▲ *MAD* #89
September 1964
ARTIST: Norman Mingo
WRITER: Staff

Universal Pictures was not pleased with this cover, threatening legal action for *MAD*'s use of the Boris Karloff version of the Frankenstein monster, the rights to which were owned by the studio. Further problems were avoided when *MAD* promised never to show that particular version of the creature on any future cover. Fortunately, we never promised we wouldn't show this cover in a book about *MAD* covers.

The monster resurfaced thirty-one years later for the cover of #334. In retrospect, both Robert De Niro and *MAD* would have been better off if they hadn't resurrected the idea.

◀ **MAD #90**
October 1964
ARTIST: Norman Mingo
WRITER: Sergio Aragonés

▼ **MAD #91**
December 1964
WRITER: Staff

▲ **MAD #92**
January 1965
ARTIST: Norman Mingo
WRITER: Staff

MAD #93
March 1965
ARTIST: Norman Mingo
WRITER: Staff
LOGO: Harvey Kurtzman

Unlike Universal's Frankenstein monster (#89), this optical illusion was (thankfully) not copyrighted. It was sent in by a reader who claimed it was his own creation. Misled, the editors bought the image and called it "The *MAD* Poiuyt"—the name was derived from reading the second row of letters on a typewriter backward. It was later discovered that the image had been in existence for quite a while, a favorite bulletin board image of engineers and physicists.

Along with Arthur the Plant and the *MAD* Zeppelin, the *MAD* Poiuyt pops up in the background of many issues.

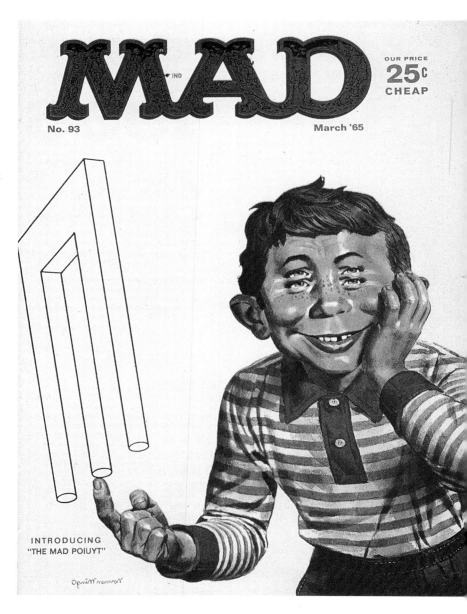

▶ **MAD #94**
April 1965
ARTIST: Norman Mingo
WRITER: Staff

A favorite movie of *MAD* publisher Bill Gaines was *King Kong* (the 1933 version). When editor Nick Meglin pencilled a rough sketch of the Alfred/Kong switch, Gaines went ape over it. Thus what began as a private joke wound up as a cover, the seventh honored as the "Soul of *MAD*."

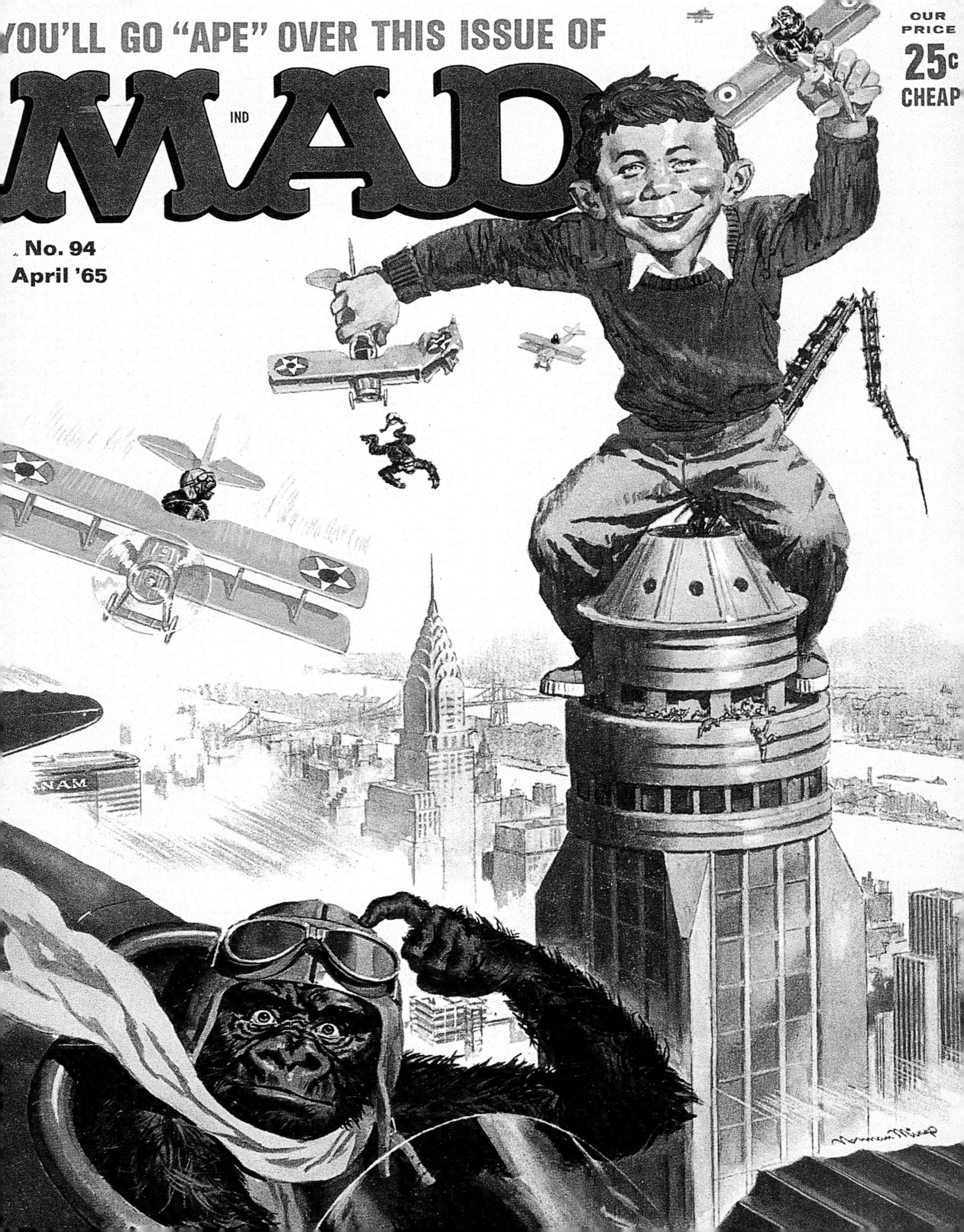
YOU'LL GO "APE" OVER THIS ISSUE OF
MAD
IND
No. 94
April '65
OUR PRICE
25c
CHEAP

MAD #95
June 1965
ARTIST: Norman Mingo
WRITER: Staff
LOGO: Harvey Kurtzman

MAD raises its price a nickel, the "Cheap" crossed out. Three years later rising costs forced up the price to "35¢—Highway Robbery." In 1971 *MAD* raised its price yet another nickel. Publisher Gaines tried to placate his readers with these successive front-cover comments: "40¢—Ouch!"; "40¢—Outrageous!"; "40¢—No Laughing Matter"; "40¢—Relatively Cheap!"; "40¢—Cheap (Considering!)"; "40¢—Cheap?"; and, finally, "40¢—Cheap."

The 40¢ price got a ten-cent boost to "50¢—Yecch!" in 1974, then nickel-and-dimed its way to $1.00 in 1982, thence to "$1.50—Bad!" in 1988, and "$1.99—Astronomical!" in 1995. As of this writing, the cover price is "$2.99—Cheap!"

Though *MAD*'s price has risen at least a dozen times, the editors proudly point out that they've never once raised the quality.

SPECIAL SPRING TRAINING ISSUE OF

NO. 95 June '65

MAD

OUR PRICE 30¢ ~~CHEAP~~

▶ **MAD #96**
July 1965
ARTIST: Norman Mingo
WRITER: Sergio Aragonés/Ilia Rubini

This is the eighth "Soul of *MAD*" honoree. The idea for the cover, a prime example of Alfred's idiocy, was submitted by Sergio Aragonés. Editor John Ficarra specifically asked to have the original Norman Mingo artwork hung in his office to serve as a daily reminder of "the quintessential Alfred visual gag cover."

THE SOUL OF MAD

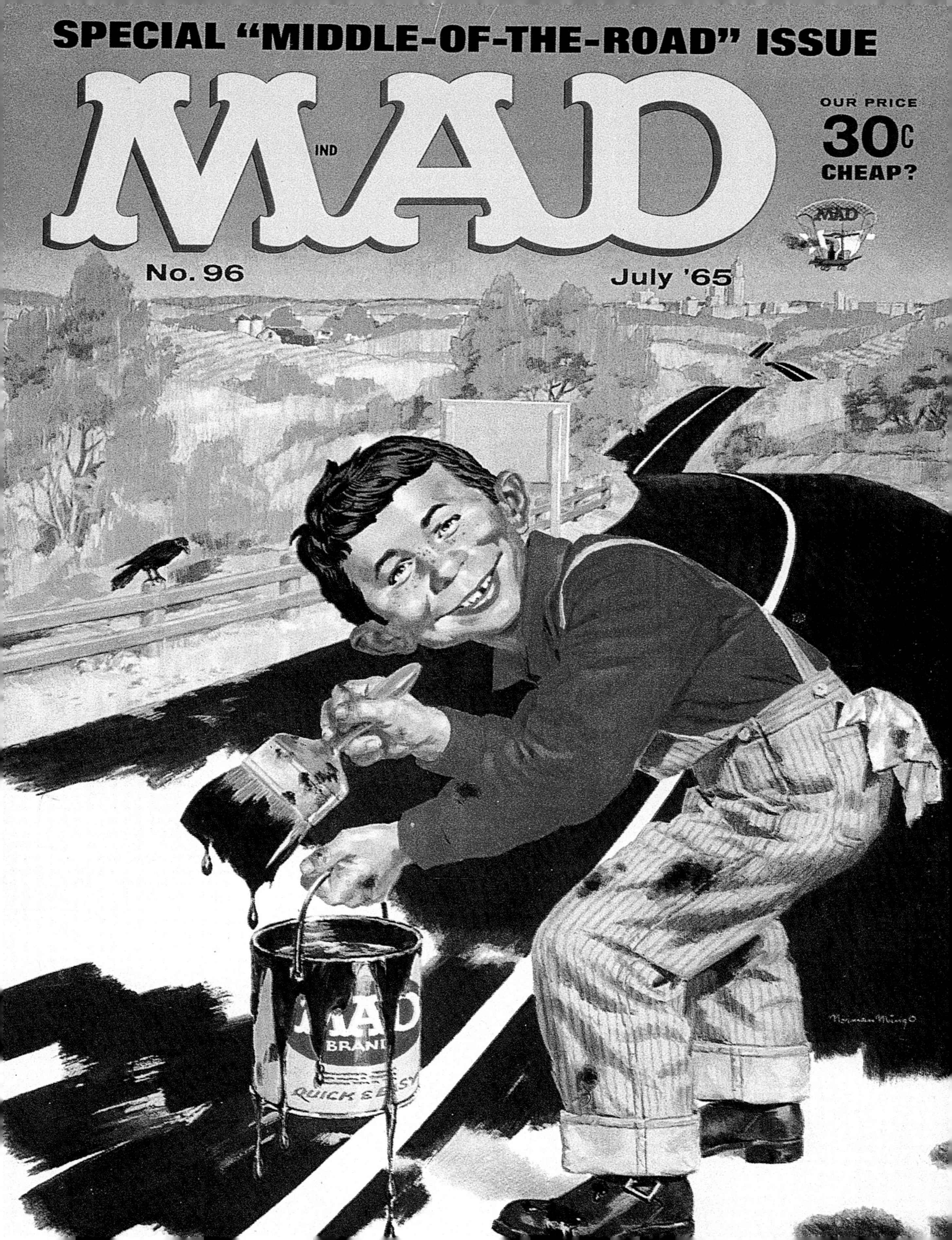

SPECIAL "MIDDLE-OF-THE-ROAD" ISSUE
MAD
IND
OUR PRICE
30¢
CHEAP?
No. 96
July '65
MAD
BRAND
QUICK & EASY

▼ MAD #97
September 1965
ARTIST: Norman Mingo
WRITER: Sergio Aragonés
LOGO: Don Martin

◀ MAD #98
October 1965
ARTIST: Norman Mingo
WRITER: Staff
LOGO: Al Jaffee

▲ MAD #99
December 1965
ARTIST: Norman Mingo
WRITER: Staff

MAD #100
January 1966
ARTIST: Norman Mingo
WRITER: Staff

No.
100

Jan.
'66

MAD
IND

OUR
PRICE
30c
CHEAP

PROUDLY PRESENTS ITS 100th ISSUE

Big deal!

Perhaps no other cover demonstrates so blatantly *MAD*'s continual self-deprecation. Through the years, the magazine has referred to its contents as trash, its pages useful for lining bird cages or wrapping fish. Whatever was implied by the celebratory gold background is quickly dashed by Alfred's comment.

► *MAD #101*
March 1966
ARTIST: Norman Mingo
WRITER: Sergio Aragonés
LOGO: Antonio Prohias

▲ *MAD #102*
April 1966
ARTIST: Norman Mingo
WRITER: Sergio Aragonés
LOGO: Sergio Aragonés

This cover within a cover within a cover "infinity" gag harkens back to the composition-book cover (#20), a device for sneaking *MAD* into class. Always a contrarian, Alfred uses *MAD* to sneak Shakespeare into class. We believe it was the Bard who said, "*A Neuman by any other name would still be as dumb.*"

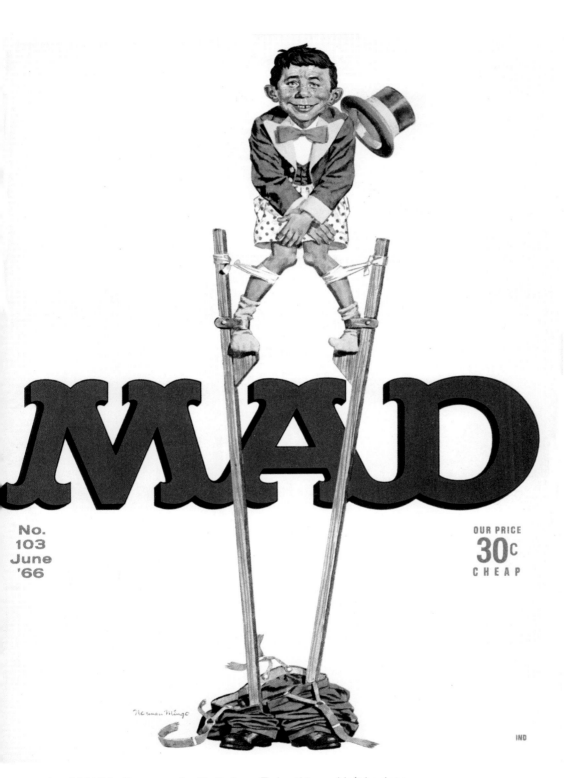

MAD #103
June 1966
ARTIST: Norman Mingo
WRITER: Sergio Aragonés

MAD

No.
103
June
'66

OUR PRICE
30c
CHEAP

IND

An example of *MAD* fooling around with its logo. Today this couldn't be done,
competition for readers' attention being so strong on the newsstand that a title must
occupy a commanding position *atop* a magazine's cover, not below the "stack" line
of the customer's vision.

SPECIAL SUMMER "CAMP" ISSUE

SPECIAL "JUNE-GROOM" ISSUE

▲ **MAD #104**
July 1966
ARTIST: Norman Mingo
WRITER: Sergio Aragonés

▶ **MAD #105**
September 1966
ARTIST: Norman Mingo
WRITER: Staff
LOGO: Bob Clarke

MAD #106
October 1966
ARTIST: Norman Mingo
WRITER: Paul Peter Porges

MAD #107
December 1966
WRITER: Gene St. Jean

MAD #108
January 1967
ARTIST: Norman Mingo
WRITER: Jerry DeFuccio

MAD #109
March 1967
ARTIST: Norman Mingo
WRITER: Antonio Prohias

Antonio Prohias, creator of "Spy vs. Spy," came up with the idea for this cover. A variation of the gag occurs on #154.

No. 110   April '67

MAD #110
April 1967
ARTIST: Norman Mingo
WRITER: Antonio Prohias

No. 111 June '67

MAD SPECIAL RACIAL ISSUE

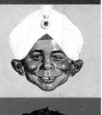

MAD #111
June 1967
ARTIST: Norman Mingo
WRITER: Staff

No. 112 July 67

MAD #112
July 1967
ARTIST: Norman Mingo
WRITER: Sergio Aragonés

MAD #113
September 1967
ARTIST: Norman Mingo
WRITER: Ziraldo

No. 113 Sept. '67

Preliminary cover concept for *MAD* #113 by Ziraldo. From the collection of Grant Geissman

MAD #115
December 1967
ARTIST: Bob Clarke
WRITER: Staff

As with #73, Publisher Bill Gaines wondered how *MAD* would sell *without* Alfred on the cover. Once again he found out with this issue (a spoof of the Avis car rental ad campaign), which sold as well as any other of the period.

#114
ber 1967
: Norman Mingo
R: Sergio Aragonés

▲ *MAD* #116
January 1968
ARTIST: Bob Clarke
WRITER: Staff

▶ *MAD* #117
March 1968
ARTIST: Norman Mingo
WRITER: Al Jaffee

◀ *MAD* #118

April 1968

ARTIST: Norman Mingo

WRITER: Staff

▲ *MAD* #119

June 1968

ARTIST: Norman Mingo

WRITER: Staff

This Norman Mingo cover was modified for Little, Brown's 1995
anthology *MAD About the Sixties* (right). Reusing this art confirms
MAD's belief in recycling. Also its world-class cheapness.

▲ **MAD #120**
July 1968
ARTIST: Norman Mingo
WRITER: Staff

▶ **MAD #121**
September 1968
ARTIST: Norman Mingo
WRITER: Staff

The Beatles have arrived and, together with Mia Farrow and their maharishi, acclaim an idiot swami. The border, with its pseudo-Sanskrit typeface, parodies the George Gershwin and Irving Caesar song "Swanee."

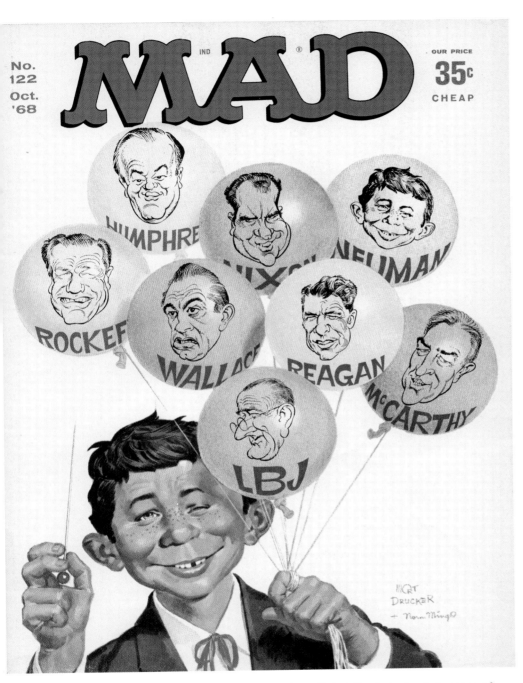

MAD #122
October 1968
ARTISTS: Norman Mingo
and Mort Drucker
WRITER: Staff

The proposed cover (right) had to be pulled at the last minute because of the assassination of Robert Kennedy. His balloon was hastily replaced by one of Alfred.

MAD #123
December 1968
ARTIST: Norman Mingo
WRITER: Staff

The number in red suggests that every copy of this issue bears a different number. In truth, only four numbers were used, but they were collated so that a buyer would have to dig down the stack five issues before realizing the gag.

THIS COPY OF

MAD

No. 123 Dec. '68

OUR PRICE 35¢ CHEAP

IS NUMBER

1,376,485

IN A SERIES OF
2,148,000

COLLECT THEM ALL!

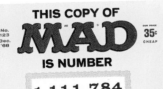

THIS COPY OF

MAD

IS NUMBER

1,111,784

IN A SERIES OF
2,148,000

COLLECT THEM ALL!

THIS COPY OF

MAD

IS NUMBER

1,189,168

IN A SERIES OF
2,148,000

COLLECT THEM ALL!

THIS COPY OF

MAD

IS NUMBER

1,112,362

IN A SERIES OF
2,148,000

COLLECT THEM ALL!

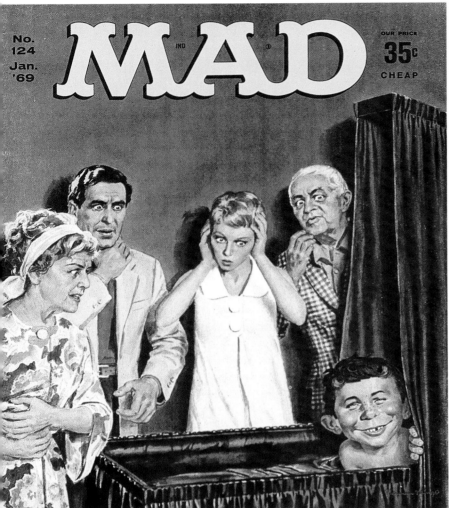

No.
124
Jan.
'69

MAD

OUR PRICE
35¢
CHEAP

IN THIS ISSUE...
Rosemia's Boo-boo

◀ *MAD* #124
January 1969
ARTIST: Norman Mingo
WRITER: Staff

WARNING! ONE MAN'S MAGAZINE
MAY BE ANOTHER MAN'S POISON

▲ *MAD* #125
March 1969
PHOTO: Irving Schild
WRITER: Staff

No. 126 April '69

MAD

OUR PRICE 35¢ CHEAP

JAMES MONTGOMERY MINGO

WHO NEEDS YOU

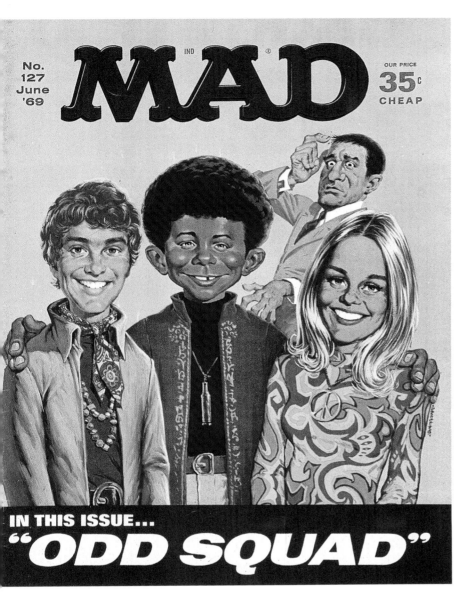

No. 127 June '69

MAD

IND

OUR PRICE 35¢ CHEAP

IN THIS ISSUE...
"ODD SQUAD"

◀ *MAD* #127
June 1969
ARTIST: Jack Rickard
WRITER: Staff

▲ *MAD* #128
July 1969
ARTIST: Bob Clarke
WRITER: Max Brandel

◀ *MAD* #126
April 1969
ARTIST: Norman Mingo
WRITER: Staff

The ninth "Soul of *MAD*" cover. When one compares this cover painting with the original poster by James Montgomery Flagg (right), the brilliance and craftsmanship of Norman Mingo become apparent.

See #48 for another cover (by Kelly Freas) incorporating the Flagg poster.

Uncle Sam by James Montgomery Flagg (1916)

MAD #129
September 1969
ARTIST: Norman Mingo
WRITER: Staff

No.
129
Sept.
'69

MAD
IND ®

OUR PRICE
35c
CHEAP

WIDENS

THE GENERATION GAP

MY
COUNTRY
RIGHT OR
WRONG

MAKE
LOVE
NOT
WAR

What would Alfred look like in middle age? The political divisiveness of the 1960s allowed readers to see the effect of the aging process—or half of it anyway.

No. 131 Dec. '69

MAD

OUR PRICE 35¢ CHEAP

BACK TO COLEGE ISUE

▲ *MAD #130*
October 1969
ARTIST: Staff
WRITER: Staff

◄ *MAD #131*
December 1969
ARTIST: Norman Mingo
WRITER: Max Brandel

Most of the mail regarding this cover dealt with the misspelling of the word "issue." The misspelling of "college" was rarely mentioned, proving the accomplished reading skills and keen attention to detail of *MAD*'s readers.

▼ **MAD #132**
January 1970
ARTIST: Norman Mingo
PHOTOGRAPHER: Lester Krauss
WRITER: Staff

No.
134
April
'70

OUR PRICE
35¢
CHEAP

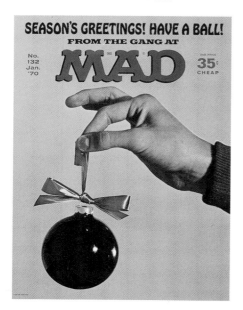

SEASON'S GREETINGS! HAVE A BALL!
FROM THE GANG AT

No.
133
March
'70

MAD 35¢
CHEAP

NO LONGER CONTAINS
CYCLAMATE
OR
M.S.G.
(Monosodium Glutamate)

ONLY
PURE, UNADULTERATED, FAT-FREE
HUMOR

◄ **MAD #133**
March 1970
ARTIST: Norman Mingo
WRITER: Dick DeBartolo

▲ **MAD #134**
April 1970
ARTIST: Norman Mingo
WRITER: Antonio Prohias

MAD #135
June 1970
ARTIST: Jack Davis
WRITER: Staff

Jack Davis returned to the covers of *MAD* with this *Easy Rider* takeoff, his first cover since #27. Davis's incredible caricatures and highly animated style always brought extraordinary energy and movement to his work. As a result, Davis was much sought after not only by *MAD*, but by Madison Avenue and by Hollywood as well.

MAD #136
July 1970
ARTIST: Norman Mingo
WRITER: Staff

No.
136
July
'70

IND MAD ®

OUR PRICE
35¢
CHEAP

IN THIS ISSUE:

BOTCH CASUALLY AND THE SOMEDUNCE KID

Butch Cassidy and the Sundance Kid (1969) featuring Katharine Ross, Robert Redford, and Paul Newman (left). Artist Norman Mingo once again displays an uncanny ability to mimic the look and palette of any original.

IN THIS ISSUE:
MAD "PUTS ON" THE DOG
(AND THE REST OF THE "PEANUTS" GANG)

A tribute to Charles Schulz's *Peanuts.* Over the years, *MAD* lampooned Charlie Brown and company in a host of articles, bringing protests from the strip's syndicate and letters of appreciation from Schulz himself. "Why don't you guys take over the whole thing, and I'll quit?" he wrote in to the magazine.

When Schulz died in February 2000, the *MAD* staff responded with one last Charlie Brown cover (#393) and an article "wrapping up" the various *Peanuts* story lines (while at the same time paying sincere tribute in their farewell to a talented friend).

MAD #139
December 1970
ARTIST: Jack Davis
WRITER: Staff

▶ **MAD #140**
January 1971
ARTIST: Norman Mingo
WRITER: Staff

George C. Scott refused to accept the Academy Award for his portrayal of General Patton (*Patton,* 1970). Alfred E. Neuman wasn't even nominated for his portrayal of George C. Scott portraying General Patton, prompting editor Nick Meglin to conclude, "The Oscars are fixed!"

No. 141 March '71

OUR PRICE 35¢ CHEAP

IN THIS ISSUE:
WE BOMB
CATCH-ALL-22

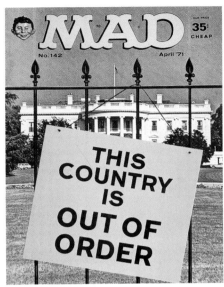

◀ **MAD #141**
March 1971
ARTIST: Jack Rickard
WRITER: Staff

▲ **MAD #142**
April 1971
ARTIST: John Putnam
WRITER: Staff

MAD #143

June 1971

ARTIST: Norman Mingo

WRITER: Staff

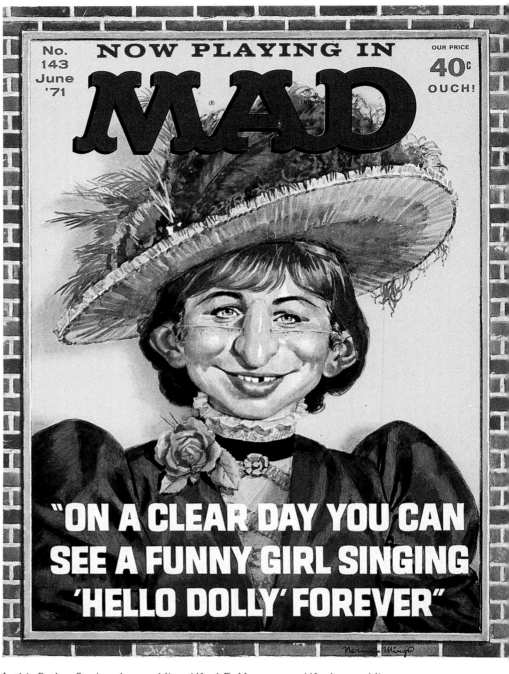

Is this Barbra Streisand resembling Alfred E. Neuman or Alfred resembling Barbra? Somehow, artist Norman Mingo brought it all off. Some say Barbra had never looked better—and Alfred had never sung worse.

MAD #144
July 1971
ARTIST: Norman Mingo
WRITER: Staff

Preliminary cover sketch for *MAD* #144 by Norman Mingo. From the collection of Alan Bernstein

MAD #145
September 1971
ARTIST: Norman Mingo
WRITER: Staff

MAD #146
October 1971
ARTIST: Norman Mingo
WRITER: Staff
LOGO: Al Jaffee

MAD #147
December 1971
ARTIST: Staff
WRITER: Staff

IN THIS ISSUE WE TEAR APART "WILLARD"

◀ *MAD* #149

March 1972

ARTIST: Jack Rickard

WRITER: Staff

▲ *MAD* #150

April 1972

ARTIST: John Putnam

WRITER: Staff

MAD #151
June 1972
ARTIST: Norman Mingo
WRITER: Staff

MAD

IND

OUR PRICE
40c
CHEAP

No.
151
June
'72
33230

M

PR

OUDLY SALUTES AMERICAN INDUSTRY IN ITS ENDLESS QUEST FOR QUALITY, ERFECTION, AND IGH STANDARDS OF PRODUCTION

P
H

TRIM
BIND

The joke was obvious to the editors, and obvious to most readers, but apparently not obvious to all newsstand dealers, some of whom were convinced the cover was a botched- up printing job. To Gaines's horror, bundles of "defective" copies were returned.

MAD #152
July 1972
ARTIST: Stan Borack
WRITER: Staff

No. 152 July '72
33230

IND MAD

OUR PRICE 40¢ CHEAP

▶ **MAD #153**
September 1972
ARTIST: Norman Mingo
WRITER: Staff

With 1972 came yet another write-in presidential campaign for Alfred. The cover didn't get him elected, but it did become the tenth "Soul of *MAD*" honoree.

Preliminary cover sketch for *MAD* #153 by Norman Mingo. From the collection of Jason Levine

No.
153
Sept.
'72

33230

MAD

IND

OUR PRICE
40¢
CHEAP

ALFRED E. NEUMAN FOR PRES

MAD

IND

No. 154 Oct. '72

33230

OUR PRICE
40¢
CHEAP

No. 155 Dec. '72 33230

MAD IND

OUR PRICE 40¢ CHEAP

IN THIS ISSUE WE BLAST... The Godfather

▲ MAD #155
December 1972
ARTIST: Norman Mingo
WRITER: Staff

▼ MAD #156
January 1973
ARTIST: Norman Mingo
WRITER: Staff

No. 156 Jan. '73

MAD IND

OUR PRICE 40¢ CHEAP

IN THIS ISSUE: "FIDDLER MADE A GOOF!"

No. 157 March '73

MAD IND

OUR PRICE 40¢ CHEAP

IN THIS ISSUE WE RIP OFF... "THE PLANET OF THE APES" AND ITS SEQUELS

▲ MAD #157
March 1973
ARTIST: Norman Mingo
WRITER: Staff

AD #154
ber 1972
T: Norman Mingo
ER: Antonio Prohias

The eleventh "Soul of *MAD*" cover. Alfred's missing tooth was often a source of inspiration, as seen on the covers of #109, #197, #236, and #263.

SOUL OF MAD

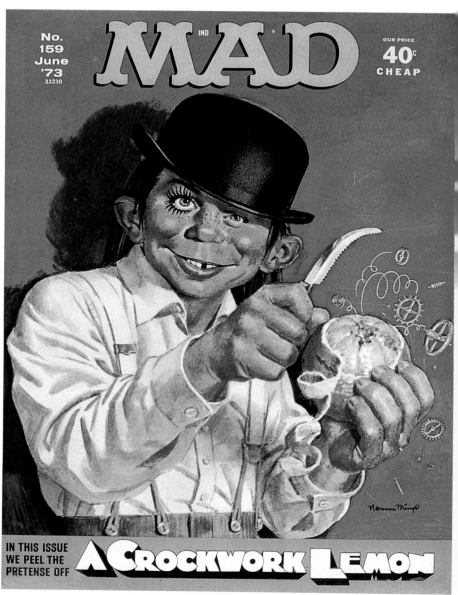

▲ *MAD* #158
April 1973
ARTIST: Norman Mingo
WRITER: Staff

▶ *MAD* #159
June 1973
ARTIST: Norman Mingo
WRITER: Staff

▼ *MAD* #160
uly 1973
RTIST: Norman Mingo
VRITER: Staff

▶ *MAD* #161
September 1973
ARTIST: Norman Mingo
WRITER: Staff
LOGO: Harvey Kurtzman

▲ *MAD* #162
October 1973
ARTIST: Norman Mingo
WRITER: Sergio Aragonés

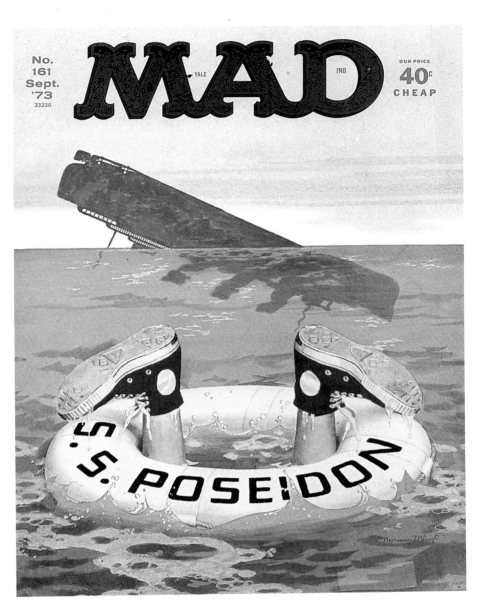

No face of Alfred, only his feet in his trademark red high-top sneakers, yet the high-water mark in sales. More than two million copies were snapped up. This premise, an homage of sorts, was reprised for the *Titanic* cover (#369).

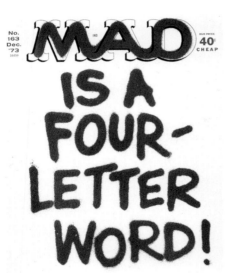

IS A
FOUR-
LETTER
WORD!

▲ *MAD* #163
December 1973
ARTIST: Staff
WRITER: Staff

▶ *MAD* #164
January 1974
ARTIST: Norman Mingo
WRITER: Staff

IN THIS ISSUE
THE TEAR APART
"PAPER
MOON"

No. 167 June '74 33230

MAD
IND

OUR PRICE 40¢ CHEAP

IN CASE OF
WORRY
BREAK OPEN
THIS ISSUE

No. 169 Sept. '74 33230 **MAD** IND OUR PRICE 40¢ CHEAP

SPECIAL COP OUT ISSUE
SERPICOOL AND McCLOD

MAD #169
September 1974
ARTIST: Mort Drucker
WRITER: Staff

No. 170 Oct. '74 33230 **MAD** IND OUR PRICE 40¢ CHEAP

THE
EXORCIST
BARF
BAG

"IF THE DEVIL MAKES YOU DO IT"

IN THIS ISSUE, WE GAG UP "THE EXORCIST"

MAD #170
October 1974
ARTIST: Bob Clarke
WRITER: Staff
LOGO: Bob Clarke

Artist Mort Drucker

▶ *MAD* #171
December 1974
ARTIST: Norman Mingo
WRITER: Staff

It was 1974 and both Richard Nixon and his deposed vice president, Spiro Agnew, were trying to con their way out of criminal offenses. Concurrently, *The Sting*, starring Paul Newman and Robert Redford, was riding high in movie houses. *MAD* took the film's memorable poster and transformed it into this Nixon-Agnew cover. Note the J. C. Leyendecker *Saturday Evening Post* motif, a pictorial hallmark of the movie, perfectly captured by the genius of artist Norman Mingo.

John Ficarra rates co-editor Nick Meglin's idea as being in many ways the finest of all four hundred covers, perhaps because of its double-barreled impact. The original art hangs in Meglin's office—the twelfth and (to date) final "Soul of *MAD*" cover, even though Alfred doesn't even appear in the painting.

THE STING

OUR PRICE

50¢

YECCH!

33230

No. 171

December 1974

MAD SALUTES
THE BIG CON

Also In This Issue We Zip ... "THE STING"

▶ **MAD #172**
January 1975
ARTIST: Norman Mingo
WRITER: Sergio Aragonés

▶▶ **MAD #173**
March 1975
ARTIST: Jack Davis
WRITER: Sergio Aragonés

▶ **MAD #174**
April 1975
ARTIST: Norman Mingo
WRITER: Staff

▶▶ **MAD #175**
June 1975
ARTIST: Norman Mingo
WRITER: Antonio Prohias

No. 176
July '75
33230

MAD

OUR PRICE
50¢
CHEAP

IN THIS ISSUE, WE SOCK AIRPORT '75!

No. 177
Sept. '75
33230

MAD

OUR PRICE
50¢
CHEAP

IN THIS ISSUE, WE SHPRITZ
THE TOWERING INFERNO

◄◄ *MAD* #176
July 1975
ARTIST: Mort Drucker
WRITER: Staff

◄ *MAD* #177
September 1975
ARTIST: Norman Mingo
WRITER: Staff

No. 178
Oct. '75
33230

MAD

OUR PRICE
50¢
CHEAP

IN THIS ISSUE WE WRECK... **GODFATHER II & ORIENT EXPRESS**

WITH THIS ISSUE...
MAD
33230
No. 179   Dec. 1975

LOWERS ITS PRICE!

MAINLY TO HERE!
50¢
CHEAP SHOT

◄◄ *MAD* #178
October 1975
ARTIST: Jack Davis
WRITER: Staff

◄ *MAD* #179
December 1975
WRITER: Staff

MAD #180

January 1976

ARTIST: Mutz (Mort Kuntzler)

WRITER: Staff

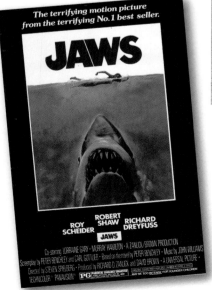

The iconic poster from the 1975 Steven Spielberg blockbuster (left). After seeing *Jaws* that summer, beachgoers everywhere were afraid to go near the water. After seeing *MAD*'s cover and reading the magazine's idiotic satire of the movie, many readers said they were afraid to go near a newsstand again.

MAD #181
March 1976
ARTIST: Norman Mingo
WRITER: Staff

MAD
No. 181 March '76
33230
OUR PRICE 50¢ CHEAP

SALUTES THE BICENTENNIAL YEAR

Dear Mr. Stuart,
I really do not believe this to be a good likeness of me! It would best remain unfinished!
G. Washington

Unfinished portrait of George Washington by Gilbert Stuart (1796)

MAD salutes the Bicentennial by Neumanizing Gilbert Stuart's unfinished portrait (above right) of George Washington (rumor has it that nausea prevented Norman Mingo from finishing Alfred's portrait!). Other covers featuring pre-*MAD* presidents include the Mount Rushmore quartet (#31), Andrew Jackson (#251), and a Neumanized Abraham Lincoln (#324). For those Calvin Coolidge fans, there are no present plans for an Alfred morph anytime soon.

▲ *MAD* #182
April 1976
ARTIST: Bob Jones
WRITER: Staff

▶ *MAD* #183
June 1976
ARTIST: Norman Mingo
WRITER: Staff

No.
183
June
'76
33230

SPECIAL "BRING BACK ARBOR DAY" ISSUE

No.
184
July
'76
33230

MAD

IND

OUR PRICE
50¢
CHEAP

◄ *MAD* #184
July 1976
ARTIST: Bob Jones
WRITER: Sergio Aragonés

▲ *MAD* #185
September 1976
ARTIST: Norman Mingo
WRITER: Staff

UNLIKE OTHER GREEDY MAGAZINES THAT EXPLOIT HOT PERSONALITIES TO SELL COPIES, WE REFUSE TO FEATURE GUESS-WHO ON OUR COVER

...EVEN THOUGH WE DO A TAKE-OFF OF "HAPPY DAYS" IN THIS ISSUE...ALONG WITH A SATIRE OF "ALL THE PRESIDENT'S MEN" FEATURING GUESS-WHO AND-WHO

▲ *MAD #186*
October 1976
ARTIST: Jack Rickard
WRITER: Staff

▶ *MAD #187*
December 1976
ARTIST: Jack Rickard
WRITER: Staff

...strikes out
**THE BAD
NEWS BEARS**

...shoots down
**MISSOURI
BREAKS**

...backhands
**THE TENNIS
CRAZE**

...needles
**DOCTORS AND
THE A.M.A.**

...and short-circuits
**THE BIONIC
WOMAN**

◄ *MAD* #188
January 1977
ARTIST: Jack Rickard
WRITER: Staff

▲ *MAD* #189
March 1977
ARTIST: Jack Rickard
WRITER: Staff

Preliminary cover sketch for
MAD #188 by Jack Rickard.
From the collection of
Michael Lerner

MAD #190
April 1977
ARTIST: Jack Rickard
WRITER: Al Jaffee

MAD #191
June 1977
ARTIST: Bob Clarke
WRITER: Staff

MAD #192
July 1977
ARTIST: Bob Jones
WRITER: Staff

MAD #193
September 1977
ARTIST: Jack Rickard
WRITER: Staff

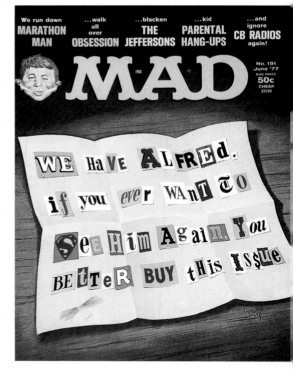

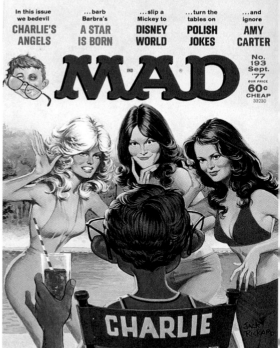

MAD #194
October 1977
ARTIST: Jack Rickard
WRITER: Staff

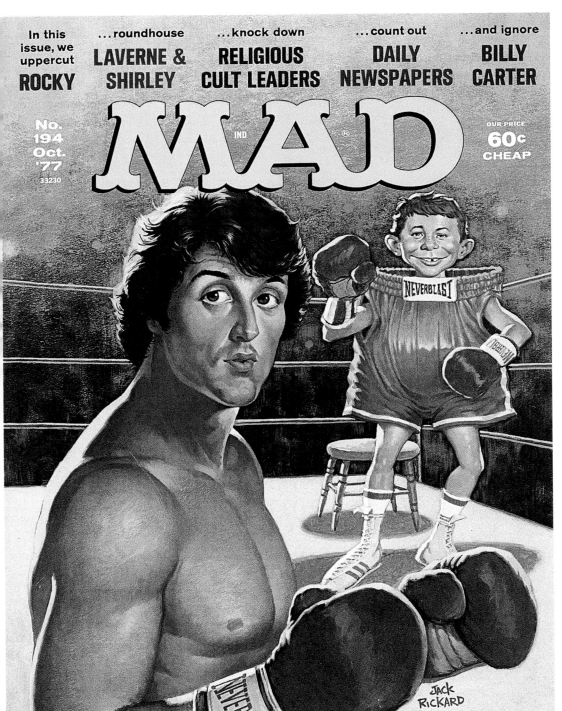

In this issue, we uppercut **ROCKY**

...roundhouse **LAVERNE & SHIRLEY**

...knock down **RELIGIOUS CULT LEADERS**

...count out **DAILY NEWSPAPERS**

...and ignore **BILLY CARTER**

No. 194 Oct. '77 33230

MAD

IND ®

OUR PRICE **60¢** CHEAP

NEVERBLAST

JACK RICKARD

Let's see, the gag here is that puny Alfred is wearing a pair of oversized trunks. Er . . . no, the gag is that of an astounded Rocky taking on an undersized opponent. No, that's not it either. The gag is that Alfred is wearing oversized trunks so that all of Rocky's punches will land *below* the belt and therefore disqualify him, thus making Alfred the winner by default. That *must* be the gag. (Wow! Talk about genius ideas!) Or maybe it's one of the best cover gags *MAD* has ever had and it's over everyone's head. Yes, that's it! On the other hand . . . Oh, let's forget it.

No.
195
Dec.
'77
33230

MAD IND ®

OUR PRICE
60¢
CHEAP

PSSST!

KEEP THIS ISSUE OUT OF THE HANDS OF YOUR PARENTS!

(MAKE 'EM BUY THEIR OWN COPY!)

▲ **MAD #195**
December 1977
WRITER: Staff

▶ **MAD #196**
January 1978
ARTIST: Jack Rickard
WRITER: Staff

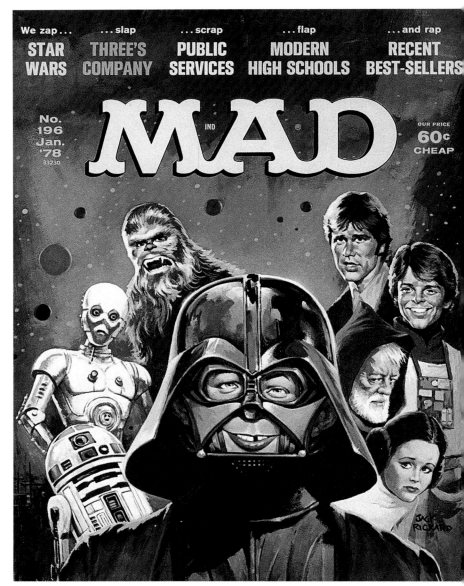

We zap... ...slap ...scrap ...flap ...and rap

STAR WARS THREE'S COMPANY PUBLIC SERVICES MODERN HIGH SCHOOLS RECENT BEST-SELLERS

No. 196 Jan. '78
33230

MAD IND ®

OUR PRICE
60¢
CHEAP

The first cover spoofing a *Star Wars* film. The original art is now owned by George Lucas. Over the years, he and Steven Spielberg have bought eleven *MAD* covers featuring their films.

MAD #197
March 1978
ARTIST: Jack Rickard
WRITER: Staff

We re-zing...   ...sting   ...wing   ...sling   ...and sing

STAR
WARS

LITTLE HOUSE
ON THE PRAIRIE

"IN SEARCH
OF..." MOVIES

PHYSICAL
FITNESS

THE CARTER
FOLLIES

No.
197
March
'78
33230

MAD

IND

OUR PRICE
60c
CHEAP

MAD #198
April 1978
WRITER: Staff

No. 198
April '78
OUR PRICE
60¢
CHEAP
33230

HOPES THIS ISSUE JAMS EVERY COMPUTER IN THE COUNTRY...

70989 33230

...FOR FORCING US TO DEFACE OUR COVERS WITH THIS YECCHY UPC SYMBOL FROM NOW ON

It would appear that no one at *The New Yorker* is a *MAD* fan. At least, that's how it seemed when, ten years after this issue appeared, their editors used an oversized UPC symbol for one of *their* covers (November 14, 1988). Surely *The New Yorker* wouldn't have *stolen* the idea. Never! Not them! They're much too sophisticated to use an idea that had appeared on the cover of a low-life magazine such as *MAD*.

EXCLUSIVE: FBI RELEASES BIONIC MAN'S FINGERPRINTS

◀ *MAD #199*
June 1978
ARTIST: Al Jaffee
WRITER: Al Jaffee

▲ *MAD #200*
July 1978
ARTIST: Jack Rickard
WRITER: Staff

MAD #201
September 1978
ARTIST: Jack Rickard
WRITER: Staff

We burn up... ...scorch ...broil ...roast ...and incinerate

"SATURDAY NIGHT FEVER" TEENAGE TACTICS BUFFET SUPPERS DISCO JOINTS "EIGHT IS ENOUGH"

No. 201 Sept. '78

MAD

IND ®

OUR PRICE 60c CHEAP

SWATCH FOR ALFRED'S AND
NEW PIN STRIPE SUIT TIE
09

In 1977 the film *Saturday Night Fever* and its soundtrack broke all records. This issue, however, broke no records and kept *MAD* barely alive.

In this issue, we give... "COMA" the treatment
... then burn SUMMER CAMPS
... mutilate BUBBLE GUM CARDS
... wreck SUMMER RESORTS
... and sink "LOVE BOAT"

No. 202 Oct. '78

MAD

IND

OUR PRICE
NÔTRE PRIX
75¢
CHEAP
PAS CHER

EXCLUSIVE:
NEW BALLISTIC TEST PROVES BOOTH DID NOT SHOOT LINCOLN

70989 33230
10

◄ *MAD #202*
October 1978
ARTIST: Jack Rickard
WRITER: Sergio Aragonés

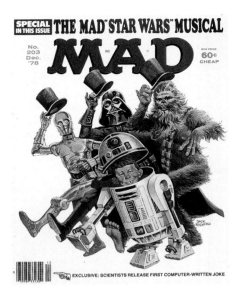

SPECIAL IN THIS ISSUE THE MAD™ STAR WARS™ MUSICAL

No. 203 Dec. '76

MAD

IND

OUR PRICE
60¢
CHEAP

JACK RICKARD

EXCLUSIVE: SCIENTISTS RELEASE FIRST COMPUTER-WRITTEN JOKE

▲ *MAD #203*
December 1978
ARTIST: Jack Rickard
WRITER: Staff

MAD #204
January 1979
ARTIST: Jack Rickard
WRITER: Staff

MAD #205
March 1979
ARTIST: Jack Rickard
WRITER: Staff

MAD #206
April 1979
ARTIST: Norman Mingo
WRITER: Staff

MAD #207
June 1979
ARTIST: Bob Jones
WRITER: Staff

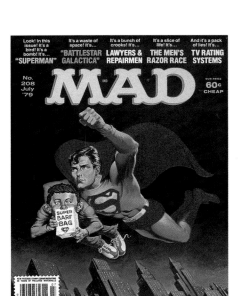

▲ **MAD #208**
July 1979
ARTIST: Jack Rickard
WRITER: Staff

▶ **MAD #209**
September 1979
ARTIST: Norman Mingo
WRITER: Al Jaffee

THE MAD "LORD OF THE RINGS" MUSICAL   OUR VERSION OF "VEGAS"   AL JAFFEE   DAVE BERG   DON MARTIN

...AND THE USUAL GANG OF IDIOTS ARE ALL IN THIS ISSUE OF...

MAD

No. 210 October '79

OUR PRICE 75¢ CHEAP

◀ *MAD* #210

October 1979

ARTIST: Sergio Aragonés

WRITER: Sergio Aragonés

▲ *MAD* #211

December 1979

ARTIST: Norman Mingo

WRITER: Staff

Preliminary cover sketch for *MAD* #211 by Norman Mingo. From the collection of Dr. Gary L. Kritzberg

Although Sergio Aragonés (who was famous for drawing the many "marginals" that appear throughout the magazine) had supplied a number of cover ideas over the years, this cover is the first one that he illustrated. Also it is one of the few instances when Norman Mingo's prototype for Alfred was not used. Protests Aragonés, "Yes it was! That's the closest I can do!"

119

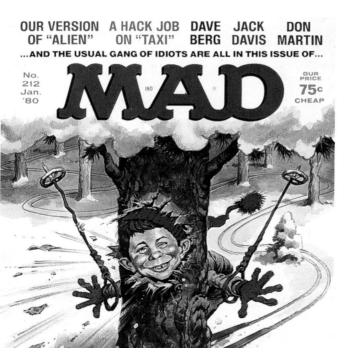

MAD #212
January 1980
ARTIST: Jack Davis
WRITER: Staff

MAD #213
March 1980
ARTIST: Jack Davis
WRITER: Staff

Preliminary cover sketch for *MAD* #213 by Jack Davis. From the collection of Joe and Nadia Mannarino

Preliminary cover sketch for *MAD* #212 by Norman Mingo, who passed away before he could begin work on the painting. From the collection of Jason Levine

Preliminary cover sketch for *MAD* #212 by Jack Davis. From the collection of Dr. Gary L. Kritzberg

▲ **MAD #214**

April 1980

WRITER: Staff

▶ **MAD #215**

June 1980

ARTIST: Bob Jones

WRITER: Staff

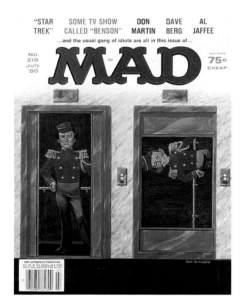

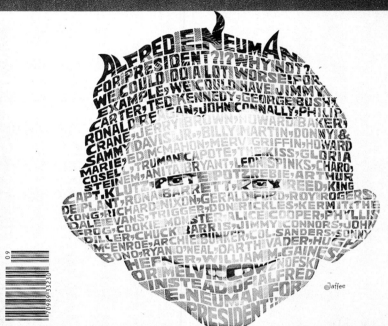

▲ MAD #216
July 1980
ARTIST: Jack Rickard
WRITER: Don "Duck" Edwing

▶ MAD #217
September 1980
ARTIST: Al Jaffee
WRITER: Al Jaffee

If this "presidential" cover had a title, it might well be called "Namely Alfred," his image made up of the names of several dozen celebrities and politicians. Among the alternative candidates: Howard Cosell, Charo, Merv Griffin, Anita Bryant, Don Rickles, Jimmy Carter, Sammy Davis Jr., Melvin Cowznofski, and someone named William M. Gaines.

Artist Al Jaffee, working with his brother Harry, did the type on a vellum overlay; Mingo's Alfred was then dropped in mechanically by the art department, creating this memorable image—and the inspiration for the back cover of the book you are now holding.

VOTE MAD
No. 218 Oct. '80
OUR PRICE 75¢ CHEAP
YOU COULD DO WORSE...AND YOU ALWAYS HAVE!

ALFRED E. NEUMAN

MAD'S "WRITE-IN" CANDIDATE FOR PRESIDENT

MAD #218
October 1980
ARTIST: Norman Mingo
WRITER: Staff

No. 219 DEC. '80 OUR PRICE 75¢ CHEAP

MAD #219
December 1980
ARTIST: Don Martin
WRITER: Don "Duck" Edwing

Preliminary cover sketch for *MAD* #220 by Jack Rickard. From the collection of Richard Landivar

"THE EMPIRE STRIKES BACK"   A DUMB TV SHOW CALLED "QUINCY"   DON MARTIN   DAVE BERG   AL JAFFEE
...and the usual gang of idiots are all in this issue of...

No. 220 Jan. '81
OUR PRICE 75¢ CHEAP

MAD #220
January 1981
ARTIST: Jack Rickard
WRITER: Don "Duck" Edwing

Preliminary cover sketch for
MAD #223 by Sam Viviano

MAD #225 back cover
ARTIST: Jack Rickard
WRITER: Staff

MAD #225
September 1981
ARTIST: Mort Drucker
WRITER: Staff

A double cover. The idea to satirize the film *Altered States* was the original choice for the front, but the popularity of *Popeye* re-altered *Altered States,* and muscled it to the rear.

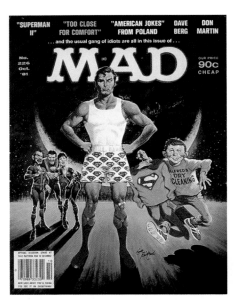

◀ *MAD* #226
October 1981
ARTIST: Jack Rickard
WRITER: Staff

▶ Preliminary cover
sketch for *MAD* #226
by Jack Rickard. From
the collection of Tom
Anderson

▶ Preliminary cover sketch for
MAD #228 by Jack Rickard. From
the collection of Jason Levine

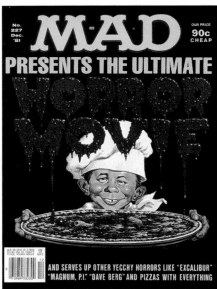

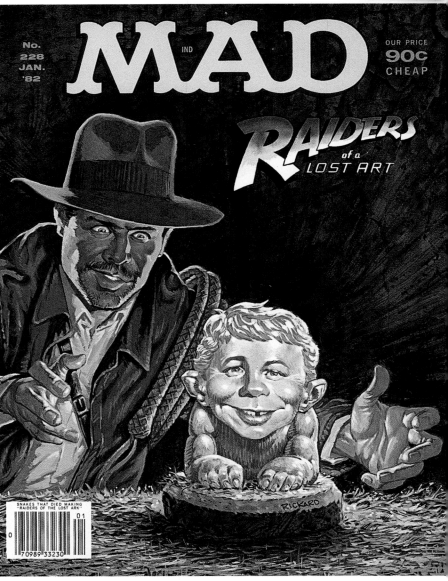

▲ *MAD* #227
December 1981
ARTIST: Jack Rickard
WRITER: Staff

▶ *MAD* #228
January 1982
ARTIST: Jack Rickard
WRITER: Staff

"FOR YOUR EYES ONLY"
"FAMILY FEUD"
SPY VS. SPY
DAVE BERG
DON MARTIN
AL JAFFEE
...and the usual gang of idiots are all in this issue of...
MAD
IND
No. 229 MARCH 1982
OUR PRICE 90¢ CHEAP
BURP!
LAST GAS FOR NEXT 200 MILES
PLAY THE MAD ACCORDION
Lesson Number 1: First, pull it apart like this! Then... push it in!
D.MARTIN..

◀ ***MAD* #229**

March 1982

ARTIST: Don Martin

WRITER: Don "Duck" Edwing

NO. 230 APRIL '82
MAD
INVADERS
OUR PRICE 90¢ CHEAP
NEW VIDEO GAMES
THE "STAR WARS" LOG
"GENERAL HOSPITAL"
THE MORAL MAJORITY
DON MARTIN
...and the usual gang of idiots invade your space in this issue

▲ ***MAD* #230**

April 1982

ARTIST: Bob Clarke

WRITER: Staff

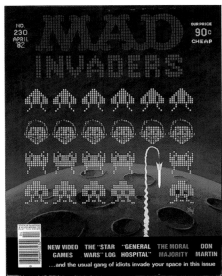

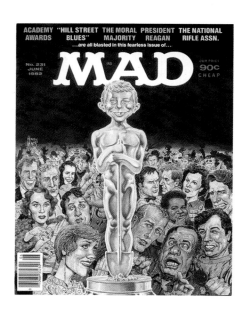

▲ MAD #231

June 1982

ARTIST: Harry North

WRITER: Staff

▶ MAD #232

July 1982

ARTIST: Jack Rickard

WRITER: Staff

MAD #233
September 1982
ARTIST: Bob Clarke
WRITER: Staff

The editors borrowed the logo of *Time* for this Pac-Man of the Year cover. They would borrow it again for #269. Some *MAD*ophiles called it a sacrilege (some lawyers called it a copyright infringement!). In any case, with the added exception of #277, the traditional logo would never again be discarded—distorted, yes, but always *MAD.*

MAD #234
October 1982
ARTIST: Mort Drucker
WRITER: Staff

ALONG WITH: DEATH CRAP · On Olden Pond · DEATH WHICH-IS-WHICH II

No. 234 Oct. '82

MAD IND ®

OUR PRICE **$1.00** CHEAP

...FINISHES OFF M*A*S*H

ARTIST'S RENDERING OF THE LAUREL & HARDY MAUSOLEUMS

DISHONORABLY DISCHARGED

Somehow, the character of Frank Burns (as played by Larry Linville) was left out of this show-'em-all *M*A*S*H* cover. "We still don't know how this happened," concedes John Ficarra. "But with the possible exception of Linville himself, nobody appeared to care."

AD #235 back cover
TIST: Boris Vallejo
RITER: Al Jaffee

MAD #235
December 1982
ARTIST: Jack Rickard
WRITER: Staff

MAD #236
January 1983
ARTIST: Jack Rickard
WRITER: Staff

MAD #237
March 1983
WRITER: Dick DeBartolo

No.
238
Apr.
'83

MAD

IND

OUR PRICE
$1.00
CHIMP

MAD #238
April 1983
ARTIST: Jack Rickard
WRITER: Staff

SALUTES CHARLES DARWIN'S BIRTHDAY*

WHAT...
ME FURRY?

HAPPY BIRTHDAY, CHARLIE!

Charles Darwin's belief in the evolution of man caused great
controversy in its time. *MAD* had no such problem, the
evolution of Alfred proving conclusively that there was no
truth to the expression "survival of the fittest."

Illustrations by Rudy
Zallinger from *Early Man*
(Time-Life Books, 1965)

133

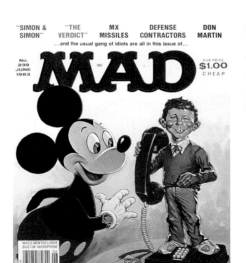

▲ *MAD* #239

June 1983

ARTIST: Jack Rickard

WRITER: Sergio Aragonés

▶ *MAD* #240

July 1983

ARTIST: Jack Rickard

WRITER: Staff

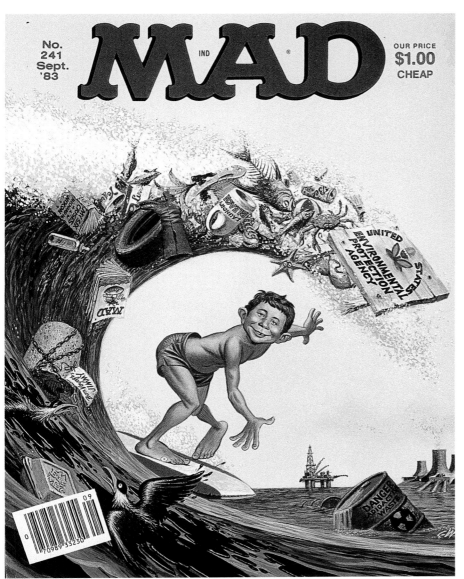

◀ **MAD #241**
September 1983
ARTIST: George Woodbridge
WRITER: Staff

▼ **MAD #242**
October 1983
ARTIST: Richard Williams
WRITER: Staff

UNMASKS "THE RETURN OF THE JEDI" AND "THE A-TEAM"

▲ Preliminary cover sketch for *MAD* #242 by Richard Williams. From the collection of John E. Hett

◀ Mark Hamill

"SUPERMAN III" IN THIS ISSUE

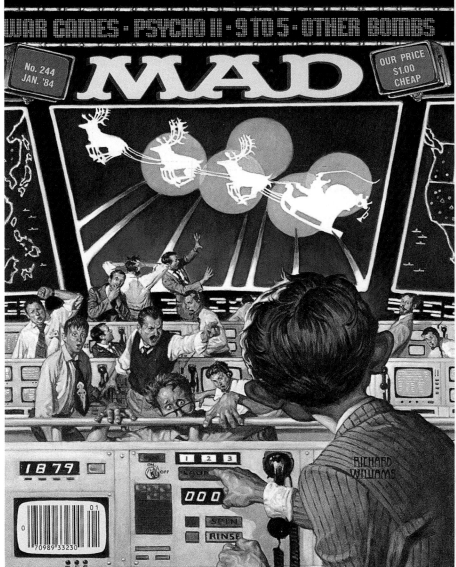

▲ *MAD #243*
December 1983
ARTIST: Richard Williams
WRITER: Staff

▶ *MAD #244*
January 1984
ARTIST: Richard Williams
WRITER: Staff

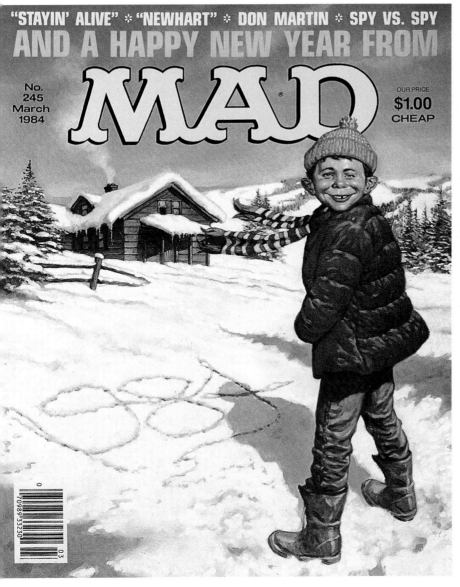

"STAYIN' ALIVE" * "NEWHART" * DON MARTIN * SPY VS. SPY
AND A HAPPY NEW YEAR FROM

MAD

No.
245
March
1984

OUR PRICE
$1.00
CHEAP

◀ **MAD #245**
March 1984
ARTIST: Richard Williams
WRITER: Staff

▲ **MAD #246**
April 1984
ARTIST: Jack Davis
WRITER: Al Jaffee

Despite opposition from the anonymous creator of this cover idea, another private office joke spills across the front cover. No longer pure as the driven snow, *MAD* relieves itself of its inhibitions and comments on the arrival of the Orwellian year 1984.

MAD #247
June 1984
ARTIST: Richard Williams
WRITER: Staff

No.
247
June
1984

MAD

IND ®

OUR
PRICE
$1.25
CHEAP

THE RIGHT STUFF?

ALSO THE WRONG STUFF LIKE...

| "AFTER MASH" | ACADEMY AWARDS | DON MARTIN | SPY VS. SPY | DAVE BERG |

"SCARFACE"*"YENTL"*"REMINGTON STEELE"*ALL GET ROASTED IN

MAD

OUR PRICE
$1.25
CHEAP

NO. 248
JULY 1984

"GREMLINS" "CHEERS" OLYMPICS DON MARTIN DAVE BERG

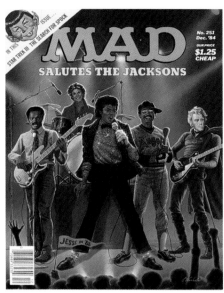

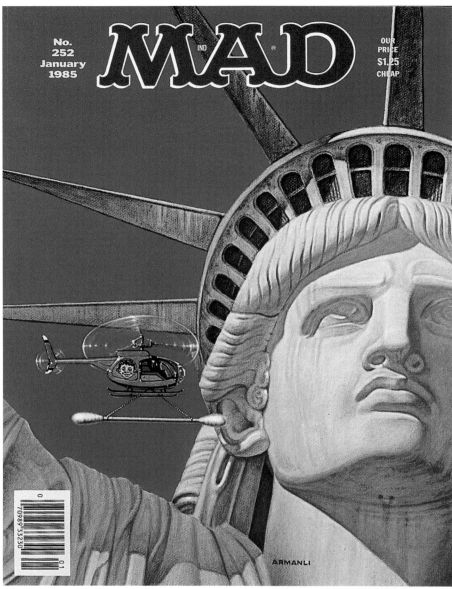

▲ **MAD #251**
December 1984
ARTIST: James Warhola
WRITER: Staff

▶ **MAD #252**
January 1985
ARTIST: Armanli (Doug Webb)
WRITER: Staff

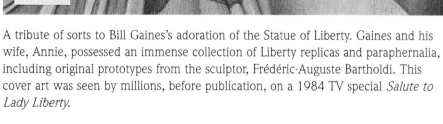

A tribute of sorts to Bill Gaines's adoration of the Statue of Liberty. Gaines and his wife, Annie, possessed an immense collection of Liberty replicas and paraphernalia, including original prototypes from the sculptor, Frédéric-Auguste Bartholdi. This cover art was seen by millions, before publication, on a 1984 TV special *Salute to Lady Liberty*.

SUPERGIRL   GHOST BUSTERS   PURPLE RAIN   THE KARATE KID

...and the usual gang of idiots are all in this issue of...

MAD

No. 253 March '85

Our Price $1.25 Cheap

YOU MAY ALREADY BE A BIG WINNER! SCRATCH OFF THESE LINES WITH A COIN AND SEE!

NEUMAN A.E.

◄ **MAD #253**

March 1985

ARTIST: Richard Williams

WRITER: Al Jaffee

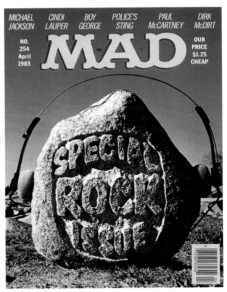

MICHAEL JACKSON   CINDI LAUPER   BOY GEORGE   POLICE'S STING   PAUL McCARTNEY   DIRK McDIRT

NO. 254 April 1985

OUR PRICE $1.25 CHEAP

MAD

SPECIAL ROCK ISSUE

▲ **MAD #254**

April 1985

PHOTOGRAPHER: Irving Schild

WRITER: Staff

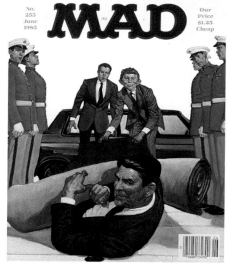

▲ **MAD #255**

June 1985

ARTIST: Richard Williams

WRITER: Al Jaffee

▶ **MAD #256**

July 1985

ARTIST: Richard Williams

WRITER: Al Jaffee

MAD #257 back cover
ARTIST: Richard Williams

MAD #257
September 1985
ARTIST: Richard Williams
WRITER: Sergio Aragonés

Preliminary cover sketch for *MAD*
#257 by Richard Williams. From the
collection of Mike Gidwitz

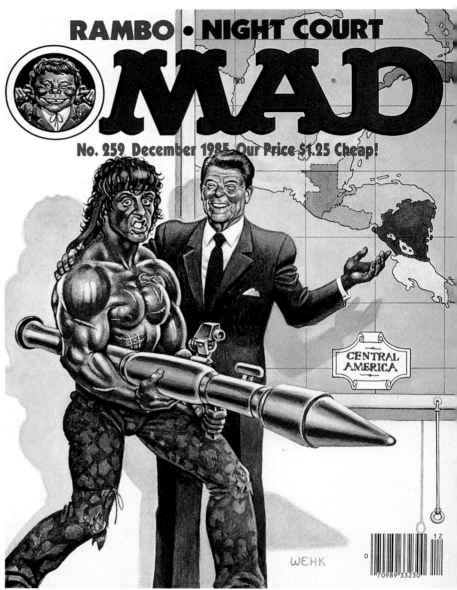

Preliminary
cover sketch for
MAD #258 by Al
Jaffee. From the
collection of
Jason Levine

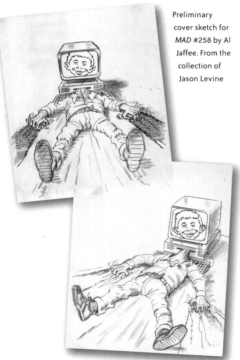

Preliminary cover sketch for
MAD #258 by Al Jaffee

▲ **MAD #259**
December 1985
ARTISTS: Will Elder and
Harvey Kurtzman
WRITER: Staff

After an absence of twenty-nine years, Harvey Kurtzman and
Will Elder are welcomed back as artists for this cover and
those of #261 and #268. Note the signature, a combination of
their initials.

THE HONEYMOONERS • COCOON

No.
260
January
~~1955~~
1980

MAD

Our
Price
$1.25
Cheap!

BACK TO THE FUTURE

1985

◀ *MAD* #260
January 1986
ARTIST: Jack Davis
WRITER: Staff

▼ *MAD* #261
March 1986
ARTISTS: Will Elder and
Harvey Kurtzman
WRITER: Staff

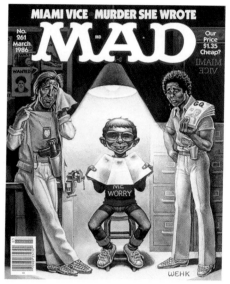

Preliminary
cover concept
for *MAD* #261
by Harvey
Kurtzman. From
the collection of
Annie Gaines

Don Johnson

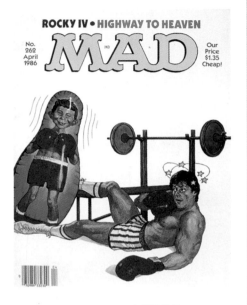

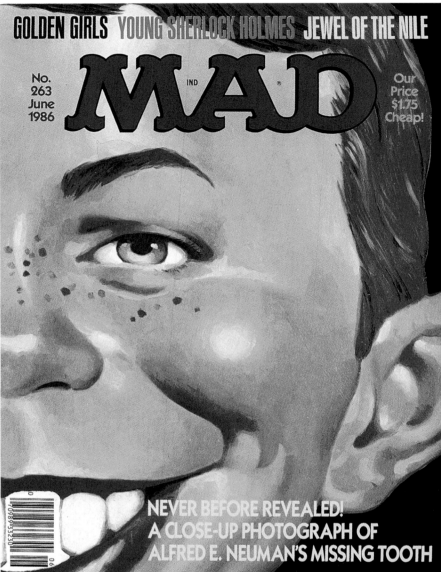

▲ **MAD #262**
April 1986
ARTIST: Richard Williams
WRITER: John Rios

▶ **MAD #263**
June 1986
ARTIST: Richard Williams
WRITER: John Rios

The ultimate in covers highlighting Alfred's missing tooth. Artist Richard Williams labored long and hard to bring off the concept. A close examination reveals the amount of subtle distortion required.

WRESTLING • RAMBO • ROCKY • MOONLIGHTING

No. 264 July 1986

MAD

Our Price $1.35 Cheap!

MAD #264
July 1986
ARTIST: Mort Drucker
WRITER: Staff

Preliminary cover sketch for *MAD* #265 by Richard Williams

DOWN AND OUT IN BEVERLY HILLS

HANNAH AND HER SISTERS

MAD

No. 265 Sept. 1986

GARBAGE PAIL ISSUE

Our Price $1.35 Disgusting!

NAUSEATING NEUMAN

MAD #265
September 1986
ARTIST: Richard Williams
WRITER: Staff

GEORGE SLAVE-OWNER — PRISSY — KHO MANIAC — DEAD MEESE — HOT AIR HELMS — WACKY KADDAFI — BULLY BOTHA — YUCKY ARAFAT — MOUTHY McENROE

MAD #265 back cover
ARTISTS: Will Elder and Harvey Kurtzman
WRITER: Staff

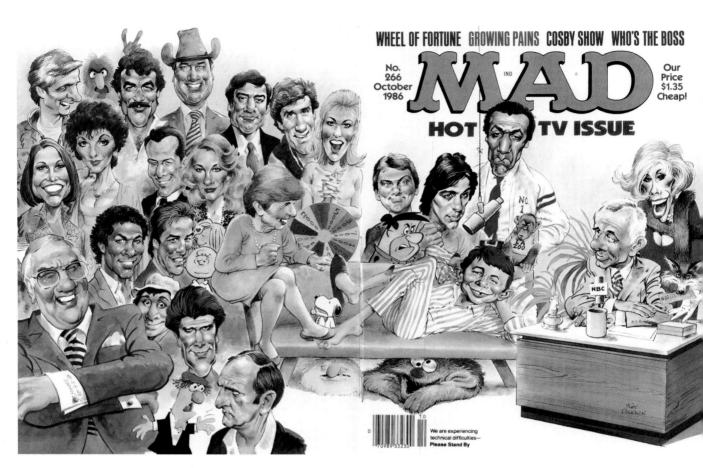

MAD #266
October 1986
ARTIST: Mort Drucker
WRITER: Staff

IN THIS ISSUE WE SHOOT DOWN TOP GUN

MAD

No. 267 December 1986

Our Price $1.35 Cheap!

DOG FIGHT

◀ *MAD* #267
December 1986
ARTIST: Richard Williams
WRITER: Staff

▲ *MAD* #268
January 1987
ARTISTS: Will Elder and Harvey Kurtzman
WRITER: Staff

Much to actress Kelly McGillis's dismay, *MAD* swapped a stud (Tom Cruise) for a dud (Alfred E. Neuman).

▲ **MAD #269**
March 1987
ARTIST: Richard Williams
WRITER: Staff

▶ **MAD #270**
April 1987
ARTIST: Richard Williams
WRITER: Staff

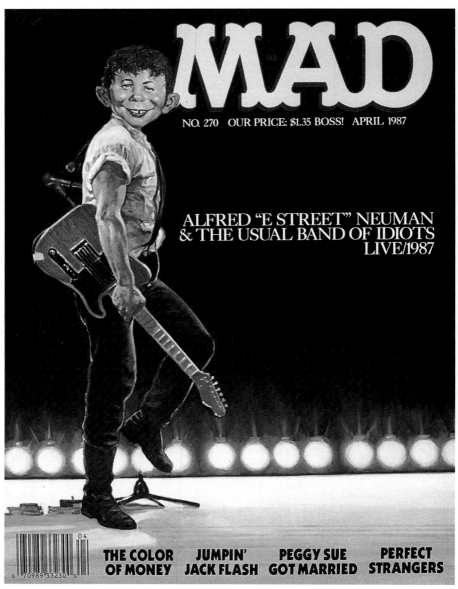

This hugely anticipated live album went on sale at midnight on November 10, 1986. Co-editor John Ficarra, not one to lose sleep over a good cover idea, first made it to the store by noon the next day and mailed a copy off to artist Richard Williams to be used as reference for the *MAD* version. The cover could not be a dead-on parody, since Bruce Springsteen was shown in profile; Alfred E. Neuman has no profile.

STAR TREK IV · THE EQUALIZER · BRUCE SPRINGSTEEN · PRO WRESTLING

No. 271
Stardate:
June
1987

MAD IND

Our
Price
$1.35
Beam It Up!

◀ **MAD #271**
June 1987
ARTIST: Richard Williams
WRITER: Staff

▼ **MAD #272**
July 1987
ARTIST: Richard Williams
WRITER: Staff

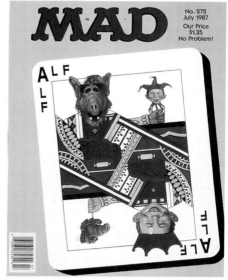

MAD No. 272
July 1987
Our Price
$1.35
No Problem!

Preliminary cover sketches for *MAD* #271
by Richard Williams. From the collection
of Mike Gidwitz

▼ *MAD* #273
September 1987
ARTIST: Richard Williams
WRITER: Staff

▶ *MAD* #274
October 1987
ARTIST: Mort Drucker
WRITER: Staff

PEE WEE HERMAN · CROCODILE DUNDEE · TV'S AMEN · DON MARTIN IN THE MORGUE · BASEBALL

No. 273 September 1987

MAD
IND

Our Price $1.35 Cheap!

Preliminary cover sketch for *MAD* #273 by Richard Williams. From the collection of Mike Gidwitz

Pee Wee Herman

L.A. LAW · NIGHTMARES ON ELM STREET · LETHAL WEAPON

MAD
IND

No. 274 October 1987 Our Price: $1.35 Cheap!

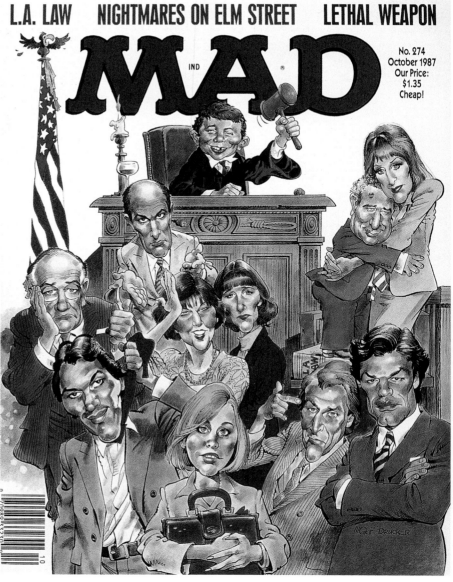

CALIFORNIA
LA LAW

Steven Bochco   August 6, 1987

MAD
Department 274
485 Madison Avenue
New York, New York 10022

Dear MAD Magazine:

Great artwork.

Great writing.

We hereby grant you by virtue of the power
vested in us by NBC and 20th Century Fox,
an honorary L.A. LAW degree.

Sincerely,

Steven Bochco

The Honorable Steven B. Bochco

SBB:mf

After seeing this cover, series creator and producer Steven Bochco sent *MAD* an unsolicited photo of the *LA Law* cast in virtually the same pose, with Bochco replacing Alfred as judge, including a blackened-out front tooth. This photo was featured on the letters page of *MAD* #276, along with a brief note (left).

▲ **MAD #275**
December 1987
ARTIST: Richard Williams
WRITER: Staff

▼ **MAD #276**
January 1988
ARTIST: Richard Williams
WRITER: Staff

BEVERLY HILLS COP II JEOPARDY DR. RUTH HEAD OF THE CLASS

No.
275
December
1987

MAD

Our
Price
$1.35
Cheap!

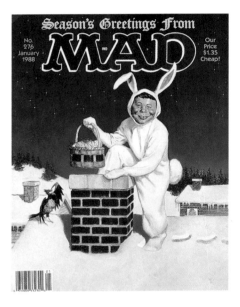

Preliminary cover sketch for *MAD* #275
by Richard Williams. From the
collection of Alan Bernstein

153

MAD #277
March 1988
ARTIST: Richard Williams
WRITER: Staff

No. 277
March 1988
Our Price
$1.50
Bad!

MAD

ALFRED E. NEUMAN

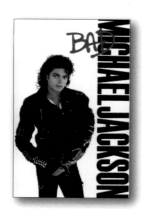

This takeoff on the Michael Jackson *Bad* album produces the same effect as that of the Streisand/Alfred cover (#143). The faces of both are immediately recognizable, although Michael/Alfred is far prettier than Barbra/Alfred.

IN THIS ISSUE WE 'RAP'...

No. 278 April 1988

MAD IND

Our Price $1.50 Cheap!

Well, howdy there, gang—get a
load...of...me—
I'm the res-i-dent id-i-ot,
Al-fred E!
MAD's' looking for suckers
who'll spend...their...cash
On this latest assortment of
mind-less...trash!
If you've time...to...waste,
then have...no...fear—
The usual gang...of...clods...
are...here!

This cover, you'll note,
is a tot-al...flop,
Guar-an-teed to make our
circ-u-lat-ion drop!
Check the movies we spoof—
you'll get...no...yuks;
"Dirty Dancing's" a dud, and
"Stake-out" sucks!
And if you need...more...
proof why hu-mor's...
died,
Take a heav-y...look at
"The Light-er...
Side"!

You should know...that...
'MAD' serves no
vi-tal...need;
Heck, the "Yel-low Pages" are
more fun...to...read!
So better wise...up, gang, and
save...your...bucks,
And you won't...wind...up
among the wimps...and...schmucks!
But if you should blow it and
you crave...the...worst—
Just remember one thing—WE WARNED YOU FIRST!

ALSO MAD PARDONS THE PRESIDENT

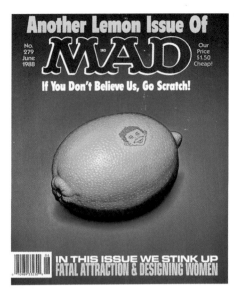

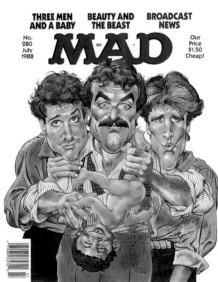

Whatever the rage, whatever the fad,
    You can bet it'll make the cover of *MAD!*
The one on issue two-seventy-eight,
    Is rap, which you either love . . . or . . . hate!
Made no difference to us how our read-ers felt,
    Just as long as they spent their hard-earned *gelt!*
Hey, it ain't . . . *MAD*'s . . . fault some rap . . . is . . . sleazy!
    Good cover ideas—they don't come easy!

MAD #281
September 1988
ARTIST: Sam Viviano
WRITER: Staff

MAD "heard it through the grapevine" that only artist Sam Viviano could fashion this memorable California Raisins cover gag (his first since *Dallas*, #223). Viviano's wide range of talents led to his becoming *MAD*'s art director in 1999.

Preliminary cover concept for *MAD* #281 by Nick Meglin (left); preliminary cover sketch by Sam Viviano (middle); preliminary color cover comp by Sam Viviano (right)

DOUBLE
DARE

STAR
TREK

BASEBALL
CARDS

ALF'S CAT
COOKBOOK

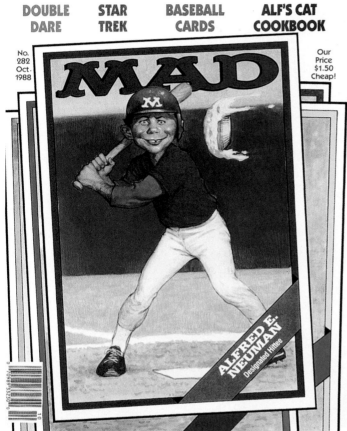

No.
282
Oct.
1988

Our
Price
$1.50
Cheap!

MAD #282
October 1988
ARTIST: Richard Williams
WRITER: Staff

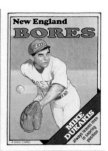

MAD #282 back cover
ARTIST: Richard Williams
WRITER: Staff

157

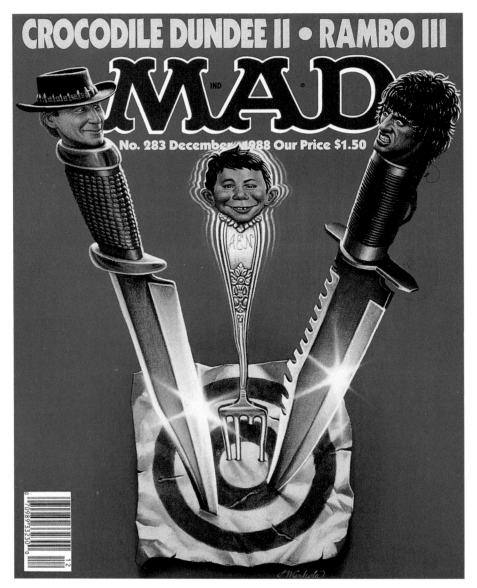

CROCODILE DUNDEE II • RAMBO III

MAD

No. 283 December 1988 Our Price $1.50

◄ **MAD #283**
December 1988
ARTIST: James Warhola
WRITER: Staff

▼ **MAD #284**
January 1989
ARTIST: Richard Williams
WRITER: Staff

ROGER RABBIT   COMING TO AMERICA   BIG

MAD

No. 284 January 1989

Our Price $1.50 Cheap!

Preliminary cover sketch for *MAD* #284 by Richard Williams. From the collection of John Hett

This dual-movie cover was the third in *MAD*'s history. Earlier the editors had combined *Murder on the Orient Express* with *The Godfather, Part II* (#178) and *Indiana Jones and the Temple of Doom* with *Splash* (#250). Co-editor John Ficarra rated them all confusing failures, leading to his formulation of the Ficarra Doctrine: "*MAD* shall never mix two movies in one gag on the same cover."

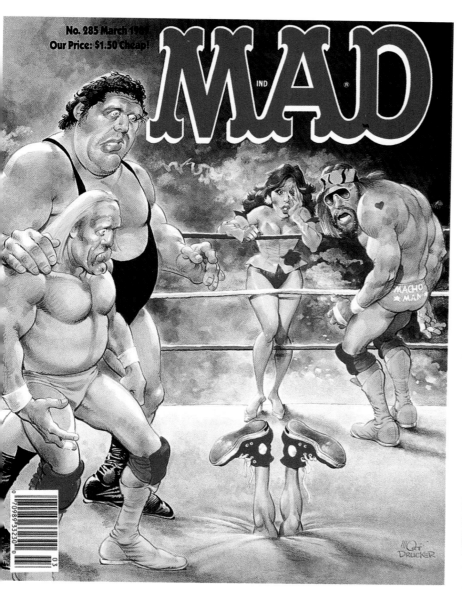

No. 285 March 1989
Our Price: $1.50 Cheap!

THIRTY-SOMETHING   THE BEATLES   MORTON DOWNEY JR.   21 JUMP STREET

No. 286 APRIL 1989   OUR PRICE $1.50 CHEAP!

SPECIAL MID-WINTER VACATION ISSUE

ROSEANNE ● WILL EISNER ● CUT-OUT BOOKMARKS
SPY VS. SPY ● ACADEMY AWARDS ● COCOON II

No. 287 June 1989   Our Price $1.50 Cheap!

159

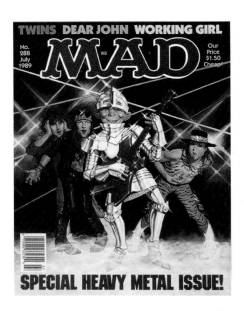

SPECIAL HEAVY METAL ISSUE!

▲ *MAD* #288
July 1989
ARTIST: Richard Williams
WRITER: Staff

▶ *MAD* #289
September 1989
ARTIST: Richard Williams
WRITER: Staff

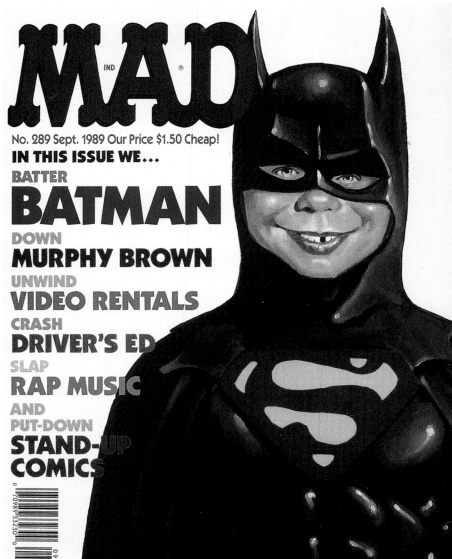

You are staring at this cover and are failing to figure out the gag. It is a wonderful gag, but you cannot find it. You are not alone. Even though you don't have X-ray vision, you try one last time, concentrating on the costume, and finally find it. Part of you experiences the thrill of discovery. The other part wishes you had spent your time more productively.

Batman was one of the hottest films of the year, prompting publisher Bill Gaines, always the joker, to make a beguiling offer: If the issue sold through more than 50 percent of its pressrun, he would take the staff to dinner at one of New York's finer restaurants. If 60 percent, he would take the staff to dinner in Paris, all expenses included. The editors, salivating, practically had their bags packed when they learned that the issue had sold 59.7 percent. Only then did they learn that Gaines had upped the pressrun for this one issue, making a 60 percent sale virtually impossible.

It was with mixed feelings that the staff sat down to their celebratory *Batman* dinner, ironically enough, at New York's Gotham Bar and Grill restaurant.

In This Issue We Shovel...
DOOGIE HOWSER & EMPTY NEST

◀ *MAD #294*
April 1990
ARTIST: Richard Williams
WRITER: Staff

▲ *MAD #295*
June 1990
ARTIST: John Caldwell
WRITER: John Caldwell

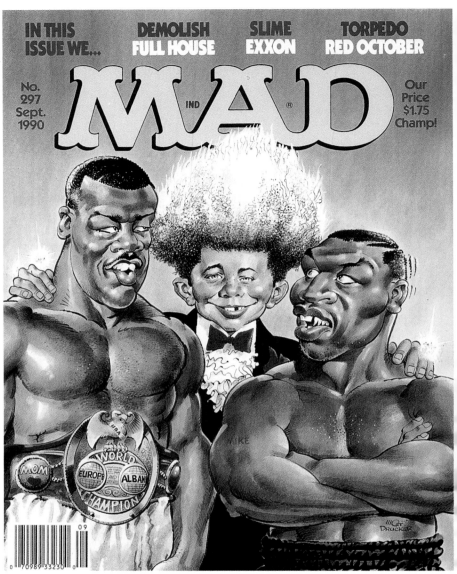

▲ *MAD* #296
July 1990
ARTIST: Jack Davis
WRITER: Staff

▶ *MAD* #297
September 1990
ARTIST: Mort Drucker
WRITER: Staff

GREMLINS II TEENAGE MUTANT NINJA TURTLES ROBOCOP II

MAD
IND

No. 298
October 1990

Our Price $1.75 Cheap!

WHAT ME WOR[RY]

◀ *MAD* #298
October 1990
ARTIST: Richard Williams
WRITER: Staff

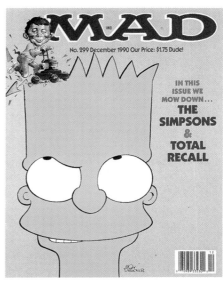

▲ *MAD* #299
December 1990
ARTIST: Mort Drucker
WRITER: Staff

MAD reader Jerry Schoen
and Matt Groenig

MAD #300
January 1991
ARTIST: Norman Mingo
WRITER: Staff

Flag burning was a hot political topic, and for *MAD*'s three hundredth issue, the editors commissioned a cover from Richard Williams depicting President George Bush burning a *MAD* flag (below), reproduced here in its entirety for the first time anywhere. The cover was headed for the presses when Saddam Hussein invaded Kuwait, resulting in Operation Desert Shield, with thousands of U.S. servicemen and women being sent to the Middle East.

After weeks of bombing Iraqi targets, it was only a matter of time before a ground war—Operation Desert Storm—would begin. *MAD*'s editors feared that when issue #300 appeared on the newsstands, the war might well be claiming the lives of GIs, with their bodies shipped home in flag-draped coffins. The cover might be looked on as being in the worst possible taste. In that light, the flag-burning cover was hastily scrapped, replaced by one utilizing Norman Mingo's classic Alfred image.

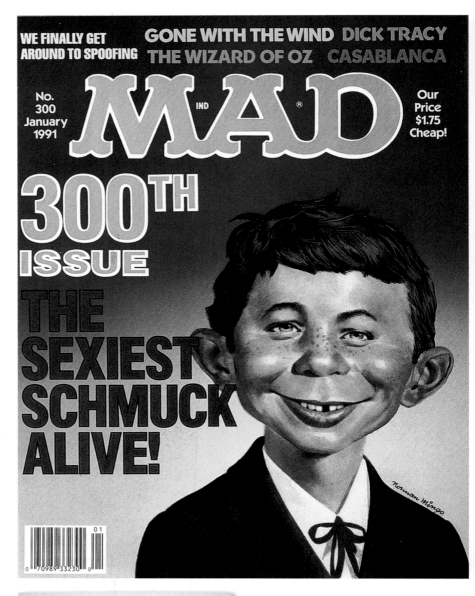

MAD #300 unused
cover art
ARTIST: Richard Williams
WRITER: Staff

MAD #301
March 1991
ARTIST: Richard Williams
WRITER: Staff

MAD #302
April 1991
ARTIST: Richard Williams
WRITER: Staff

MAD #303
June 1991
ARTIST: Mort Drucker
WRITER: Staff

During the Gulf War, special editions of #300–303 were sent gratis to servicemen and women in the Middle East. For each of these special Saddam "Hussein Asylum" editions, the UPC symbol was replaced by Alfred as Lawrence of Arabia, lifted from the cover of #86.

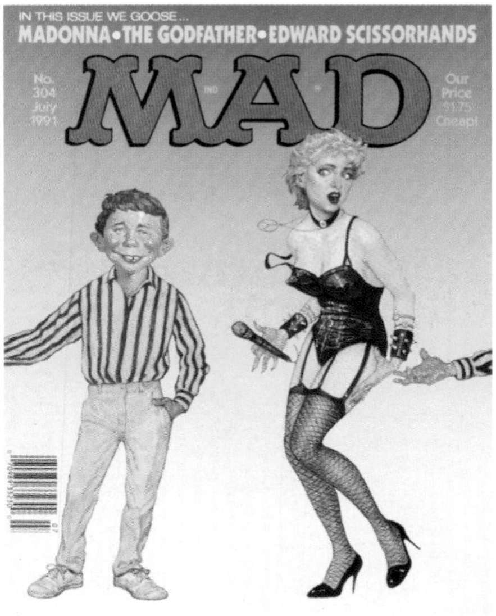
IN THIS ISSUE WE GOOSE...
MADONNA•THE GODFATHER•EDWARD SCISSORHANDS
No. 304 July 1991
MAD
Our Price $1.75 Cheap!

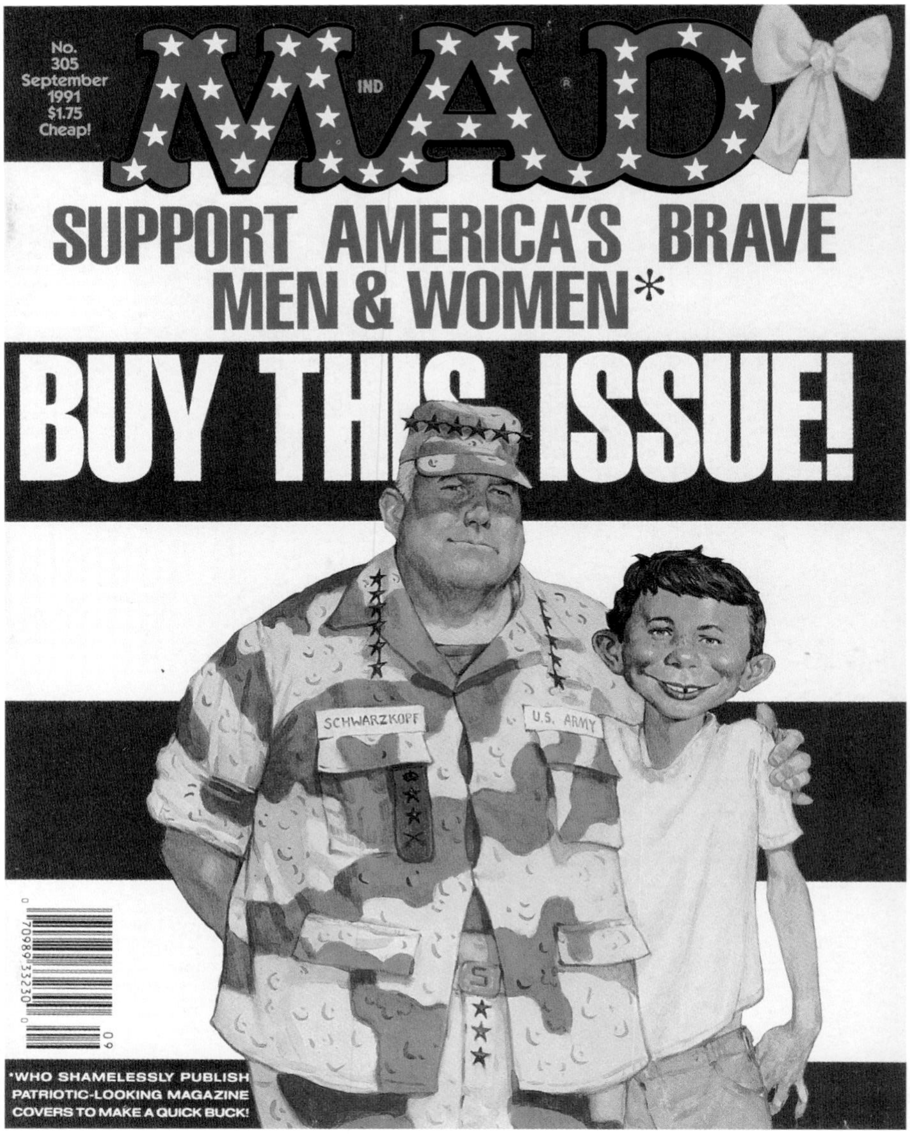
No. 305 September 1991 $1.75 Cheap!
MAD
SUPPORT AMERICA'S BRAVE MEN & WOMEN*
BUY THIS ISSUE!
SCHWARZKOPF
U.S. ARMY
*WHO SHAMELESSLY PUBLISH PATRIOTIC-LOOKING MAGAZINE COVERS TO MAKE A QUICK BUCK!

▲ ***MAD* #304**
July 1991
ARTIST: Richard Williams
WRITER: Paul Sollicito

▶ ***MAD* #305**
September 1991
ARTIST: Richard Williams
WRITER: Staff

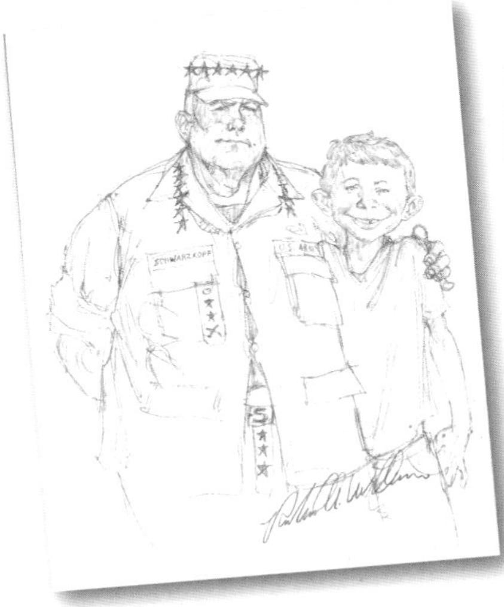

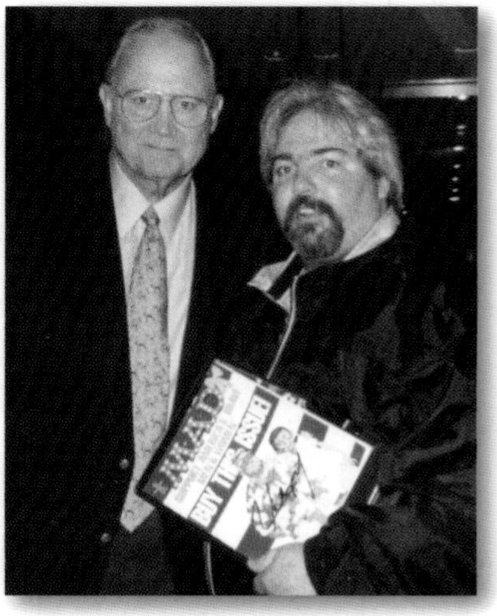

▲ Preliminary cover sketch for *MAD* #305 by Richard Williams

▶ *MAD* reader Mickey Zippo and General Norman Schwarzkopf

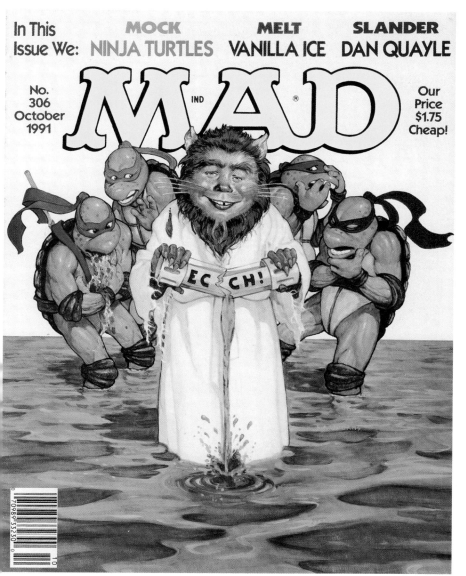

In This
Issue We:
**MOCK
NINJA TURTLES**
**MELT
VANILLA ICE**
**SLANDER
DAN QUAYLE**

No.
306
October
1991

MAD IND

Our
Price
$1.75
Cheap!

ECCH!

Preliminary cover sketch for *MAD* #307
by Richard Williams. From the collection
of Alan Bernstein

169

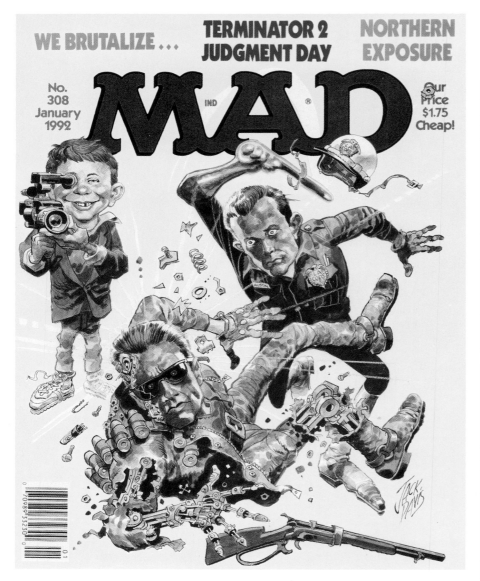

WE BRUTALIZE... **TERMINATOR 2 JUDGMENT DAY** NORTHERN EXPOSURE

No. 308 January 1992

MAD
IND

Our Price $1.75 Cheap!

A failed attempt at editorializing and one that could be called a pictorial mixed metaphor. The idea was to comment on the infamous Rodney King beating, with the Terminator being the victim of a police beating, and Alfred a bystander videotaping the incident. So why is this dud of a premise singled out here? Hey, even Michael Jordan threw up an occasional brick, though at *MAD* the brick is more often the rule than the exception.

◀ *MAD* #308
January 1992
ARTIST: Jack Davis
WRITER: Staff

▼ *MAD* #309
March 1992
ARTIST: Jack Davis
WRITER: Tom Hachtman

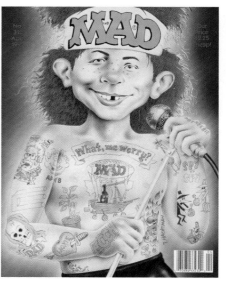

▲ *MAD* #310
April 1992
ARTIST: Tom Hachtman
WRITER: Tom Hachtman

THE ADDAMS FAMILY HOME IMPROVEMENT

No. 311
June 1992

Our Price $1.75 Cheap!

◀ **MAD #311**
June 1992
ARTIST: Richard Williams
WRITER: Staff

▼ **MAD #312**
July 1992
ARTIST: Richard Williams
WRITER: Staff

WE PUKE FUN AT **PRINCE OF TIDES**
BUGSY   HOOK
No. 312 July 1992 Our Price $1.75 Nauseating!

SCRATCH 'N' SNIFF COVER!

BARF BAG ONE
VEECH! DON'T READ HIS LIPS!
MADE IN JAPAN

The Addams Family serves up seven different Alfreds—far from the record fifteen seen on covers #298 and #387. The art shows off the talents of Richard Williams, *MAD*'s most prolific cover illustrator in the late 1980s and into the 1990s.

Preliminary cover sketch for *MAD* #311 by Richard Williams. From the collection of Ken Hawk

Artist Richard Williams.
Photo by Gosia Williams
(January 2000)

171

HEY DUMMIES! TEST DRIVE THIS ISSUE OF...

No. 313 September 1992

MAD

Our Price $1.75 Cheap!

A classic cover in all respects, especially as a vehicle for Alfred. His idiocy long a given, the premise comes off at once. Note the placement of the UPC symbol—a prime example of *MAD*'s quest for any detail, any nuance, any pun that will embellish a cover.

◀ *MAD* #313
September 1992
ARTIST: Richard Williams
WRITER: Staff

▼ *MAD* #314
October 1992
ARTIST: Mort Drucker
WRITER: Staff

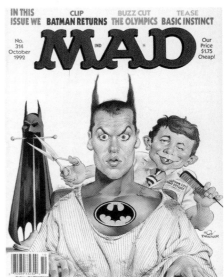

▲ *MAD* #315
December 1992
ARTIST: Mort Drucker
WRITER: Staff

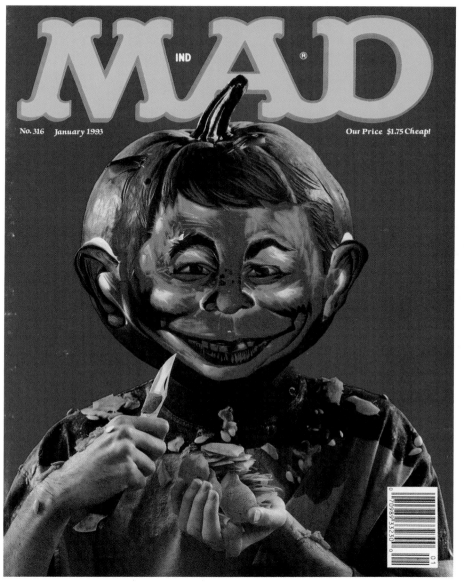

◀ *MAD* #316
January 1993
PHOTOGRAPHER: Irving Schild
SCULPTOR: Hugh McMahon
WRITER: Staff

▲ *MAD* #317
March 1993
ARTIST: James Warhola
WRITER: Staff

A difficult cover to produce and, because of the magazine's lead time, one that was created a year in advance. Sculptor Hugh McMahon carved the pumpkin to achieve the Alfred image. Then a lightbulb was placed inside the pumpkin to give it a proper glow. Photographer Irving Schild had to snap fast, as the heat of the bulb was rapidly cooking—and distorting—the shape of the pumpkin. The body, incidentally, belongs to then–assistant editor Andrew Schwartzberg, whose own half-baked head has been glowing ever since.

▼ **MAD #318**
April 1993
ARTIST: Richard Williams
WRITER: Staff

▶ **MAD #319**
June 1993
ARTIST: Richard Williams
WRITER: Staff

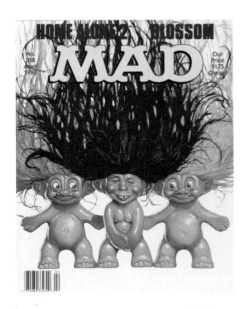

Preliminary cover sketch for *MAD* #318
by Richard Williams. From the
collection of Jason Levine

MAD #320
July 1993
ARTIST: Al Jaffee
WRITER: Al Jaffee

In 1964 *MAD*'s Al Jaffee surveyed the double and triple foldouts in magazines such as *Playboy* and *Life* and decided that *MAD* should feature its own cut-rate version. Thus was born the *MAD* Fold-In, which has graced the inside back cover of almost every issue since #86.

Pictured here is the sole Fold-In *front* cover. Nearly all the veteran freelancers are named, alongside the magazine's most heralded icons—Arthur the Plant, the *MAD* Poiuyt, the *MAD* Zeppelin, the black and white spies from "Spy vs. Spy," and numerous other images. Oh, yes, and the first cover mention of the ubiquitous and mysterious Max Korn.

Artist/writer Al Jaffee. Photo by
Charles Kochman (March 1999)

Preliminary cover sketch
for *MAD* #320 by Al Jaffee

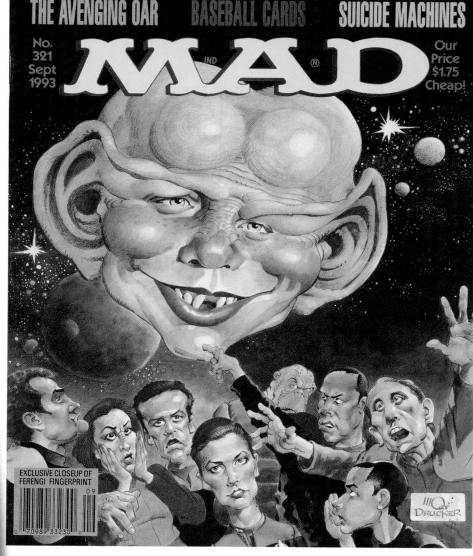

MAD #321
September 1993
ARTIST: Mort Drucker
WRITER: Staff

"DEEP SPACE SWINE"

Former President George Bush and his wife Barbara . . . oh, no, wait a minute! We mean *Star Trek: Deep Space Nine* actors Mark Allen Shepherd as Morn, left, and Armin Shimerman as Ferengi Quark delight in seeing MAD #321, which includes our satire of their program. Later, the pair were seen tossing the issue down a nearby worm hole . . . coincidence??

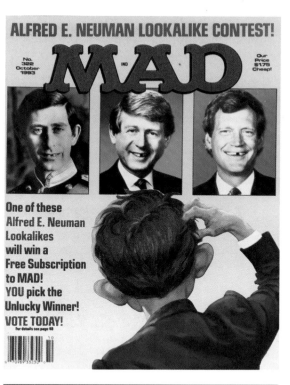

MAD #322
October 1993
ARTIST: Richard Williams
PHOTOS: AP/Wide World

The editors were convinced that Ted Koppel would win this contest in a landslide. But David Letterman led in the voting until the last week, when a torrent of ballots from Canada poured in, making Prince Charles the winner.

In the 1950s *MAD* printed a photo of the young prince that many people thought bore a striking resemblance to Alfred. Soon thereafter the magazine received a blistering rebuttal from London. Art director John Putnam, an expert in such matters, scrutinized the letter, envelope, and postmark and concluded that Prince Charles had indeed written the letter.

It seems that *MAD*'s Canadian readers have long memories, eh?

Preliminary cover sketch for *MAD* #323 by Richard Williams. From the collection of Mike Gidwitz

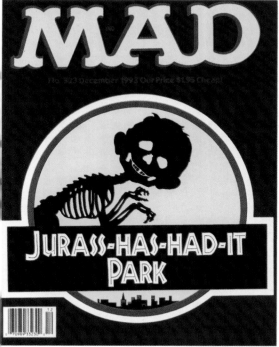

A split run, colored to mimic the two movie posters created for *Jurassic Park.*

MAD #323
December 1993
ARTIST: Richard Williams
WRITER: Staff

MAD #324
January 1994
ARTIST: Richard Williams
WRITER: Staff

Preliminary cover sketch for *MAD* #324 by Richard Williams. From the collection of Mike Gidwitz

MAD #325
February 1994
ARTIST: Sam Viviano
WRITER: Desmond Devlin

Clinton and Gore as Beavis and Butt-Head. Not the most flattering of portraits, yet diligent reader Ron Kaye got the prez and his veep to sign the cover (below right). Most likely, they wanted to show they could take a joke. Huh-huh-huh!

◄ Preliminary cover sketch for *MAD* #325 by Sam Viviano

▼ **MAD #326**

March–April 1994

ARTIST: Richard Williams

WRITER: Don "Duck" Edwing

▶ **MAD #327**

May 1994

PHOTOGRAPHER: Irving Schild

COMPUTER GRAPHICS: Peter Sun

MODEL: Tim Jackson

WARDROBE: Regina Schild

WRITER: Charlie Kadau

In 1994 Howard Stern and Rush Limbaugh were the two hottest yakkers on the radio, and both had books on the *New York Times* best-seller lists. This cover replicates the format of Stern's autobiographical best-seller, with Rush replacing Howard. Sales of the issue unfortunately were not as large as Limbaugh's waist or Stern's ego. How low were the actual sales figures? About the same as Alfred's IQ!

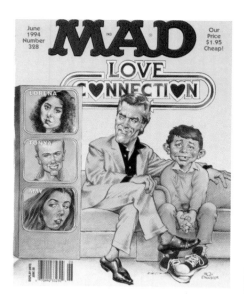

▲ MAD #328
June 1994
ARTIST: Mort Drucker
WRITER: Mike Snider

▶ MAD #329
July–August 1994
ARTIST: Mort Drucker
WRITER: Staff

The editors challenged *NYPD Blue* producer Steven Bochco to photograph the cast as they appeared on this cover. *MAD* felt that it was not an unreasonable request, since Bochco had photographed the stars of *LA Law* as they appeared on the cover of #274. Bochco respectfully declined, perhaps preferring to have his cast expose themselves only on network TV.

MAD #330
September 1994
ARTIST: Richard Williams
WRITER: Staff

A tribute to Slash, lead guitarist of Guns N' Roses, whose after-hours partying had been well publicized. In a phone call to *MAD,* he revealed a different side. Recalls co-editor Ficarra: "He came off as the nicest, most easygoing guy. Of all the magazine covers he'd been on, he said this was the only one he sent to his mother."

Slash

The brilliance of caricaturist Mort Drucker shines in this swipe at Bill Clinton and his entourage. This was *MAD*'s second song lyric cover. Alas, the song's writer exhibited a Stone Age knowledge of politics, predicting a "one term" Clinton presidency.

◀ **MAD #331**
October–November 1994
ARTIST: Mort Drucker
WRITER: Staff
LYRICS: Frank Jacobs

▼ **MAD #332**
December 1994
ARTIST: Drew Friedman
WRITER: Staff

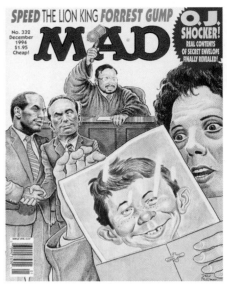

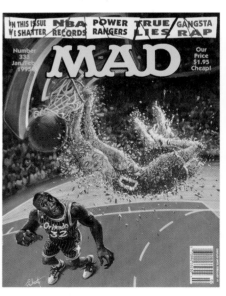

▲ **MAD #333**
January–February 1995
ARTIST: Thomas Fluharty
WRITER: Desmond Devlin

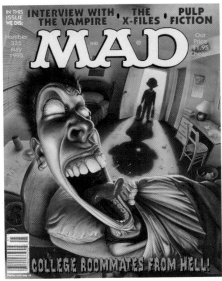

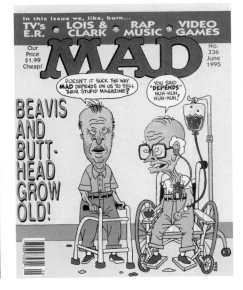

MAD #334
March–April 1995
ARTIST: Richard Williams
WRITER: Staff

MAD #335
May 1995
ARTIST: Mark Fredrickson
WRITER: Staff

MAD #336
June 1995
ARTIST: Sam Viviano
WRITER: Staff

Preliminary cover sketch for
MAD #336 by Sam Viviano

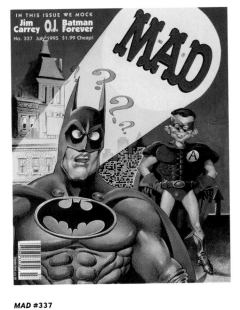

MAD #337
July 1995
ARTIST: Mort Drucker
WRITER: Staff

MAD #338
August 1995
ARTIST: Frank Frazetta
WRITER: Staff

MAD #339
September 1995
ARTIST: Jack Davis
WRITER: Staff

Preliminary cover rough for
MAD #339 by Nick Meglin

This cover led to co-editors Meglin and Ficarra being guests on Howard Stern's
radio program (August 29, 1995), which included the following exchange:

STERN: If someone had said to me when I was a little kid that one day I would be on the cover of *MAD* Magazine, it would have been unthinkable. If somebody said to me, "You'd go to the moon," I would have sooner believed that than to believe that I could be on the cover of *MAD* Magazine. To me, *MAD* was the epitome, and if somebody made it to the cover of *MAD* Magazine they had truly arrived. There isn't a performer today whose career and ideas and sense of humor, anybody in comedy, that cannot say that they were not shaped by *MAD* Magazine.

FICARRA: They will not say that.

STERN: They will not say that? Then I'm not going to say it either. But I gotta tell you something, I really could not believe it when I saw the cover. I began to shake.

MEGLIN: Howard, you have no taste, that's why.

STERN: How was the decision made to put me on the cover? Was it strictly, "Hey, Howard's got a lot of fans and maybe that'll sell a lot of magazines," or was there something more to it?

MEGLIN: Just the opposite, I would think.

FICARRA: Who the hell are we kidding? We figured you had a lot of listeners—maybe they'd buy the issue.

STERN: Well thanks for putting me on the cover—it's a true honor. This is a really big deal to me. I was on the cover of *Time* magazine—that meant nothing to me. But here I am getting my head plunged into a toilet by Alfred E. Neuman.

MEGLIN: Pulled out, pulled out.

STERN: It's being pulled out?

MEGLIN: I think it's subject to interpretation, like most of our stuff. It works on several levels.

FICARRA: None of them good.

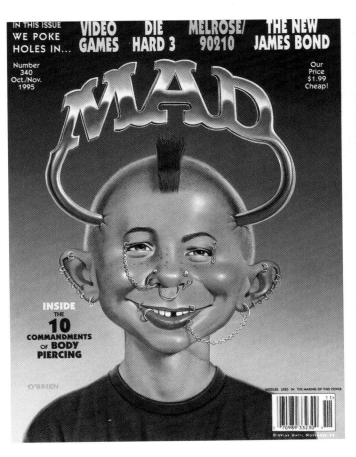

MAD #340
October–November 1995
ARTIST: Tim O'Brien
WRITER: Tom Cheney

MAD #341
December 1995
ARTIST: Vincent DiFate
WRITER: Staff

Of all the original art that has arrived at the *MAD* offices over the years, this is the only cover art that has been either stolen or lost behind a file cabinet. If you stole this artwork, please return it, no questions asked; concerned readers can otherwise show up with a couple of husky friends to help move some file cabinets.

Alfred as the Man on the Moon. The idea had been tossed around for years and at last the staff came up with an appealing premise. Comments Ficarra: "This is the only known rendering of a brown moon in the history of art." So much for the green-cheese theory!

Ron Howard

▲ **MAD #342**
January–February 1996
ARTIST: James Bennett
WRITER: Sergio Aragonés

▶ **MAD #343**
March 1996
ARTIST: Richard Williams
WRITER: Staff

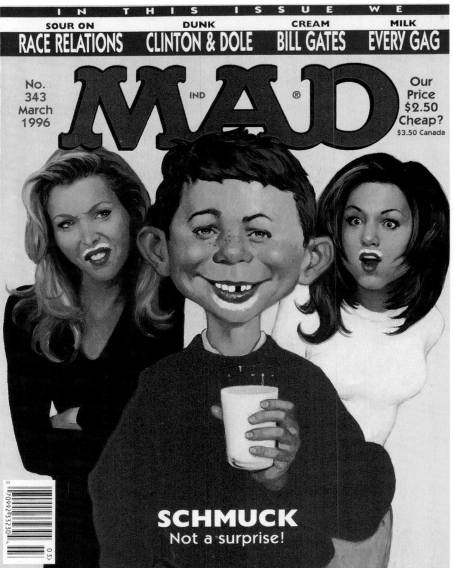

A spin on the popular ad campaign using celebrities and milk. *MAD* decided to incorporate Alfred alongside "friends" Lisa Kudrow and Jennifer Aniston, knowing the Milk Board would never select him as an example of what drinking milk can do for you.

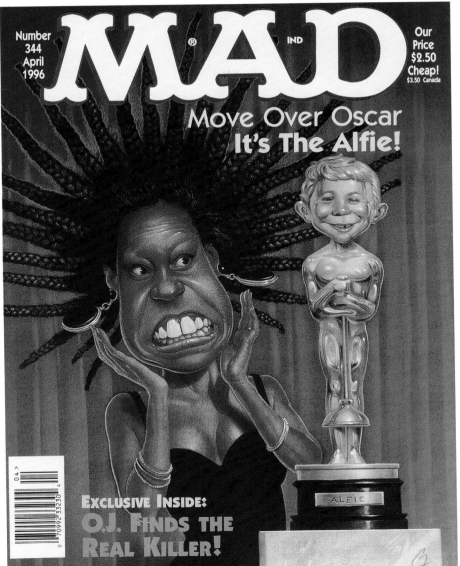

Number 344 April 1996

MAD

® IND

Move Over Oscar
It's The Alfie!

Our Price $2.50 Cheap!
$3.50 Canada

EXCLUSIVE INSIDE:
O.J. FINDS THE REAL KILLER!

0 70992 33230 4 04 >

◀ *MAD #344*
April 1996
ARTIST: C. F. Payne
WRITER: Staff

▼ *MAD #345*
May 1996
ARTIST: Richard Williams
WRITER: Sergio Aragonés

IN THIS ISSUE WE TAKE CHEAP SHOTS AT... THE BEATLES DEVIL WORSHIPPING CAROLINE IN THE CITY THE POPE

MAD
No. 345 May 1996

Our Price $2.50 Cheap! Canada $3.50

CONGRATULATIONS CLASS OF '96

By The Way, **You're DOOMED!**

We're Here, We're Stupid, Get Used To It!

MAD
No. 346 June 1996

Our Price $2.50 Cheap! $3.50 Canada

▶ *MAD #346*
June 1996
ARTIST: Joe DeVito
WRITER: Michael Gallagher

MAD reader Dave Gallo
and Whoopi Goldberg

Preliminary cover concept for
MAD #346 by Michael Gallagher
(left); preliminary cover sketch
by Joe DeVito (middle);
preliminary color cover rough
by Joe DeVito (right)

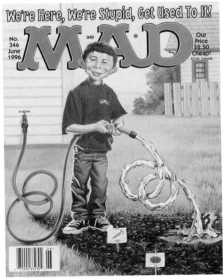

▼ **MAD #347**
July 1996
ARTIST: C. F. Payne
WRITER: Paul Peter Porges

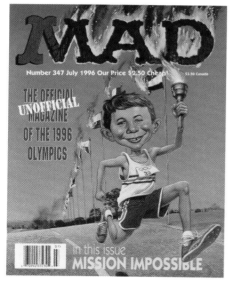

▲ **MAD #349**
September 1996
ARTIST: C. F. Payne
WRITER: Staff

A very pregnant Madonna gets an inside look at her baby-to-be. By now Alfred had been seen in various ages (#129) and stages (#238). Now we see him in his earliest state, with Madonna preparing to give birth to a less-than-immaculate misconception.

▲ **MAD #348**
August 1996
ARTIST: Mort Drucker
WRITER: Staff

◀ Preliminary cover concept for *MAD* #348 by Nick Meglin

▶ Preliminary cover concept for *MAD* #349 by Nick Meglin (left); preliminary cover rough by Joe Orlando (right)

MAD #350
October 1996
ARTIST: Richard Williams
WRITER: Staff

To celebrate its 350th issue, this magazine came polybagged with a free CD-ROM, "*MAD* Bytes It!" (right), created in conjunction with America Online and Rhino Records. Cover artwork by Mort Drucker.

▼ **MAD #351**
November 1996
ARTIST: Mark Fredrickson
WRITER: Sergio Aragonés

▶ **MAD #352**
December 1996
ARTIST: Mort Drucker
WRITER: Staff

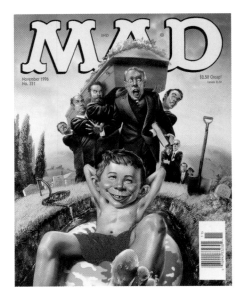

Preliminary cover rough for
MAD #351 by Mark
Fredrickson. From the
collection of Mike Gidwitz

NBA bad boy and perennial wacko Dennis
Rodman would score on this cover and #357.
Shaquille O'Neal was slam-dunked on #333.
Yet somehow Michael Jordan, the greatest
basketball player in history, would never be so
"honored." "It wasn't the first time we
dropped the ball," laments Ficarra. "And
surely it won't be the last."

Promotional issue, given
away by Tang (1997)

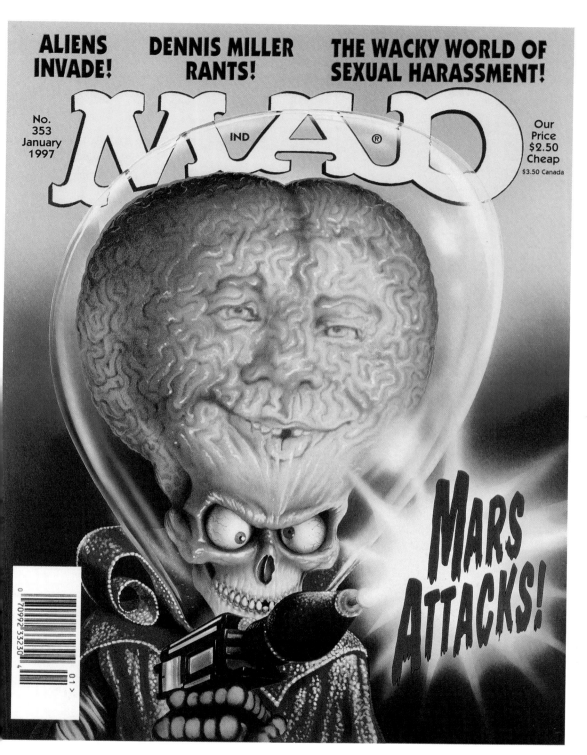

MAD #353
January 1997
ARTIST: Mark Fredrickson
WRITER: Staff

ALL NEW! **STAR WARS** UPDATED!

MAD

No. 354
February
1997

Our
Price
$2.50!
Cheap!

In This Issue...

RANSOM!
Star Wars MACARENA
Beavis & Butt-head Go HOLLYWOOD!

▲ **MAD #354**
February 1997
ARTIST: Richard Williams
WRITER: Staff

▶ **MAD #355**
March 1997
ARTIST: Richard Williams
WRITER: Staff

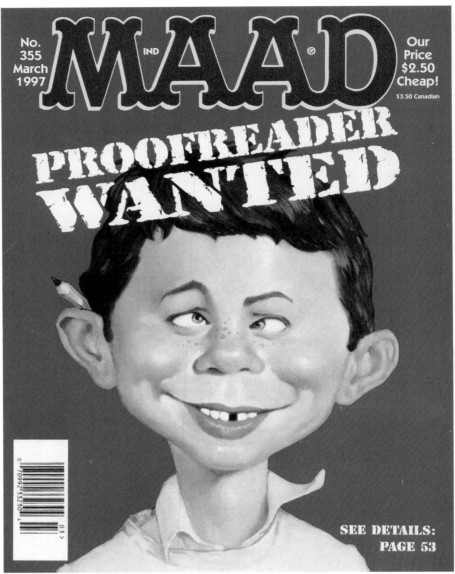

No.
355
March
1997

IND

MAAD

®

Our
Price
$2.50
Cheap!

$3.50 Canadian

PROOFREADER WANTED

SEE DETAILS:
PAGE 53

MAD reader Andy Kaufman and
Vice President Dan Quayle

The gag was there, and in plain view. The challenge was to find it. Most readers, including this writer, missed it completely. Hint: Check out the logo.

According to "Ed" of the infamous *MAD* letters page, Hans Brickface, noted "logographer" of Brickface's Bric-a-Brac, deemed this collector's issue a rarity because of the "error" and appraised it at $3,000. Was Brickface red? Not really. The letter was a joke, especially on the many *MAD* readers who wrote in!

One canny subscriber, Andy Kaufman, managed to snap a photo of Mr. Potatoe Head himself, former Vice President and International Punchline Dan Quayle, holding the issue. *MAD* published the photo (left), which Ficarra considers the ultimate "celebrity snap."

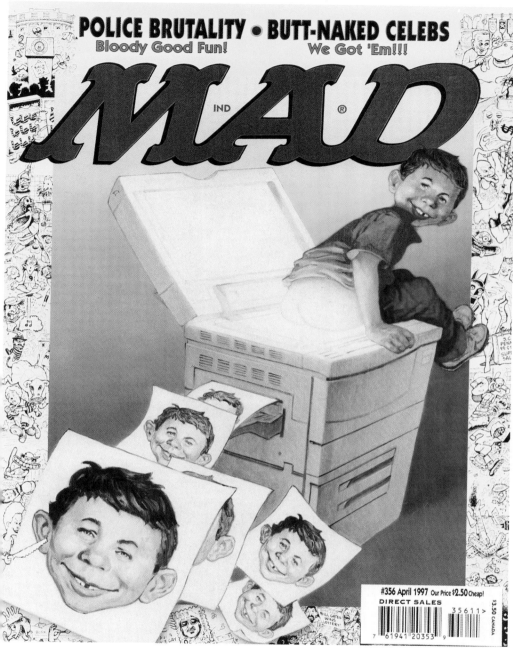

MAD #356
April 1997
ARTIST: Richard Williams
WRITERS: Tom Broderidge and Lisa Dumond
BORDER ARTIST: Tom Bunk

Preliminary cover rough for *MAD* #356
by Richard Williams. From the
collection of Mike Gidwitz

MAD brings back its cover border, with mixed results. Because the border was always yellow, some news dealers were confusing each issue with the previous one. Eventually a test was conducted in certain regions of the country, with three issues published with and without the border (#363, #364, #365). The borderless issues sold at least 15 percent better, so it was discarded with issue #370, thus ending "yellow border journalism" with a loud dud!

It was with this April Fool's issue (#356), that *MAD* was relaunched in 1997 and made "edgier," its covers and editorial content sometimes testing the boundaries of good taste.

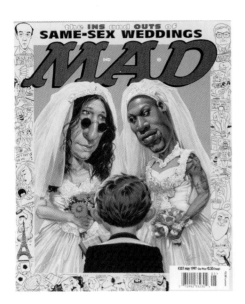

▲ *MAD* #357

May 1997

ARTIST: C. F. Payne

WRITER: Staff

BORDER ARTIST: Rick Tulka

▶ *MAD* #358

June 1997

ARTIST: Drew Friedman

WRITER: Staff

BORDER ARTIST: Sergio Aragonés

MAD #359
July 1997
ARTIST: Mort Drucker
WRITER: Staff
BORDER ARTIST: Paul Coker

After noting that *TV Guide* was printing multiple covers for the same issue, *MAD*'s editors (no dummies, they!) foisted their "cheap gimmick" on the reading public. Collectors had to buy all four to complete the appropriate epithet. A number of readers did just that, resulting in a marked increase in sales.

HOT SUMMER ISSUE!
AOL • ROSIE O'DONNELL • DRUGS • CON AIR

▲ *MAD* #360
August 1997
ARTIST: James Bennett
WRITER: Staff
BORDER ARTIST: John Caldwell

▶ *MAD* #361
September 1997
ARTIST: Sam Viviano
WRITER: Staff

A classic cover—that is, if you're not an admirer of Bill Clinton. And possibly even if you are. This is a premise for which the yellow border serves a necessary purpose. It could be argued that no *MAD* cover has made a stronger political statement. It is a true bashing across (or around) the board.

Preliminary cover rough for
MAD #361 by Nick Meglin

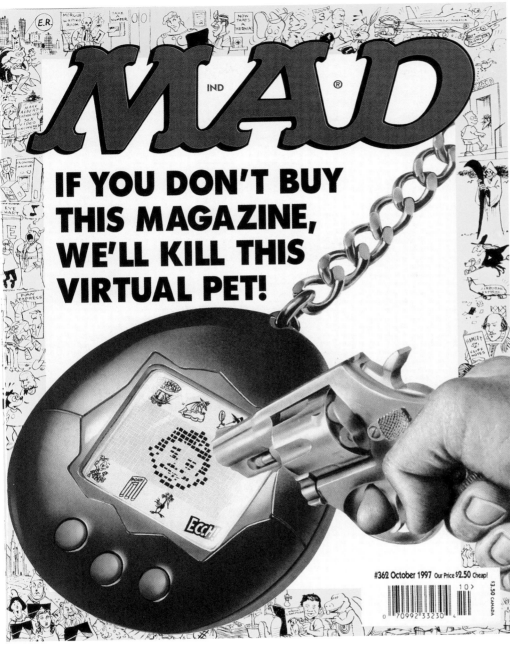

MAD #362
October 1997
ARTIST: Mark Fredrickson
WRITER: Staff
BORDER ARTIST: Angelo Torres
BORDER WRITER: Don "Duck" Edwing

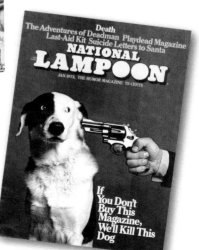

In January 1973, the *National Lampoon* published its most memorable cover (right). The cover of *MAD* #362 was conceived as both a salute to *Lampoon* and a comment on our emerging high-tech society. In the border you'll find Alfred reading that original issue of the *Lampoon*, evidence that when *MAD* lifts a premise it at least gives credit (unlike *The New Yorker* and #198). "Homage legitimizes plagiarism," claims co-editor Meglin.

MAD #363
November 1997
ARTIST: Joe DeVito
WRITER: Staff
BORDER ARTIST: Al Jaffee
BORDER WRITER: Don "Duck" Edwing

▲ Preliminary cover concept for
MAD #363 by Joe Orlando

▶ Artist Joe DeVito. Photo by
Charles Kochman (August 1999)

Artist Joe DeVito thought that he'd sold the original art for this cover to the Spice Girls. But at the last moment they demurred, feeling it cast them in an unflattering light, the poor darlings. Geri Halliwell (right), aka "Ginger" Spice, left the band shortly after. Coincidence? We think not.

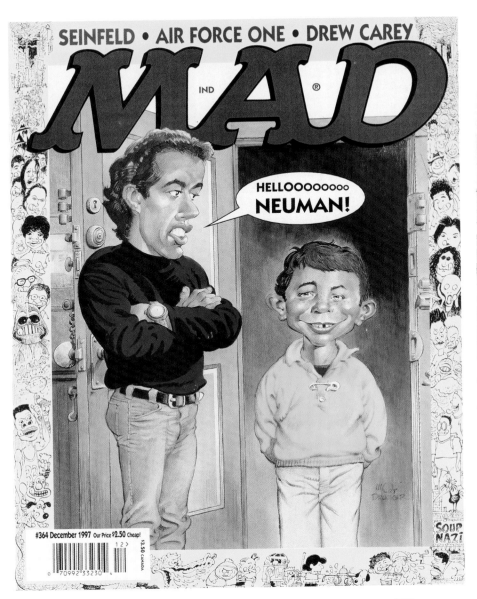

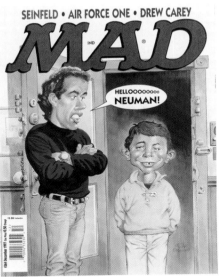

MAD #364
December 1997
ARTIST: Mort Drucker
WRITER: Staff
BORDER ARTIST: Paul Coker

A joke almost too good to be true. The nemesis of the title character on TV's most successful sitcom was named Newman. This was a cover waiting to happen. DC Comics bought the original art from Mort Drucker, the cover artist, and gave it as a present to Jerry Seinfeld, who at the time was preparing an American Express commercial featuring Superman.

MAD #365
January 1998
ARTIST: Joe DeVito
WRITER: Staff
BORDER ARTIST: Rick Tulka

MAD #366
February 1998
ARTIST: Mort Drucker
WRITER: Staff
BORDER ARTIST AND WRITER: John Caldwell

NHRA (National Hot Rod
Association) promotional
giveaway for the inaugural run
of the *MAD* Funny Car (1998)

Preliminary color cover
rough for *MAD* #365 by
Joe DeVito

BILL CLINTON'S POP-UP VIDEOS

WINTER OLYMPICS

MAD

IN THIS ISSUE WE SLAY BUFFY!

#367 March 1998 Our Price $2.50 Cheap!

0 70989 33230 0

$3.50 CANADA

03 >

MAD #367
March 1998
ARTIST: Joe DeVito
WRITER: Staff
BORDER ARTIST: Tom Bunk
BORDER WRITER: John Caldwell

ONE LINE OF INCREDIBLE COPY GOES HERE!

MAD

MAD

Preliminary cover concept for *MAD* #367 by Nick Meglin (top); preliminary cover sketch by Joe DeVito (bottom)

MAD #368
April 1998
ARTIST: Roberto Parada
WRITER: Staff
BORDER ARTIST: Monte Wolverton
BORDER WRITER: Michael Gallagher

MAD #369
May 1998
ARTIST: Mick McGinty
WRITER: Staff
BORDER ARTIST: Angelo Torres
BORDER WRITER: Don "Duck" Edwing

A pair of covers that had their genesis years earlier: #368 is reminiscent (kind of) of the stop sign cover on #47. The *Titanic* cover harkens back to #161 and *The Poseidon Adventure.*

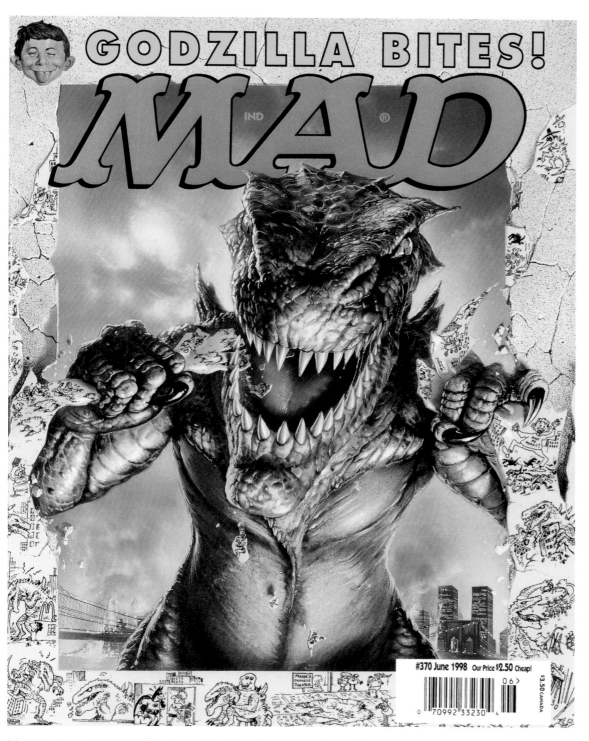

MAD #370
June 1998
ARTIST: Mark Fredrickson
WRITER: Don "Duck" Edwing
BORDER ARTIST AND WRITER:
Sergio Aragonés

Much to the relief of *MAD*'s editors, Godzilla chews up the last of the yellow borders (and apparently Alfred E. Neuman, who is nowhere to be seen). Each item in the border, rendered by Sergio Aragonés, is some kind of Godzilla gag. Anyone familiar with Sergio's work knows that size does *not* matter.

MAD #371
July 1998
ARTIST: Sam Viviano
WRITER: Desmond Devlin

Why two *South Park* covers? Purely a business decision, based on the popularity of the show and the knowledge that some collectors *must* own every issue, including variations.

The "cut paper" covers were rendered on computer by Sam Viviano, soon to take over as *MAD*'s art director.

Preliminary cover concept for *MAD* #371 by Nick Meglin (left); preliminary cover rough by Sam Viviano (right)

MAD #372
August 1998
ARTIST: C. F. Payne
WRITER: Don "Duck" Edwing

MAD #373
September 1998
ARTIST: James Bennett
WRITER: Staff

Preliminary cover
concept for *MAD* #373
by Nick Meglin

MAD #374
October 1998
ARTIST: Roberto Parada
WRITER: Staff

MAD #375
November 1998
ARTIST: Sam Viviano
WRITER: Staff

Preliminary cover
concept for *MAD* #375
by Sam Viviano

American Gothic by
Grant Wood (1930)

Over the years this classic painting by
Grant Wood (left) has been the source of
much parody and inspiration in the
magazine. To great effect, cover artist
Roberto Parada labored to achieve not
just the pose and setting but also the
morphed faces of X-Files stars Gillian
Anderson and David Duchovny with the
painting's original subjects.

▲ **MAD #376**
December 1998
ARTIST: Mort Drucker
WRITER: Ryan Pagelow

▶ **MAD #377**
January 1999
ARTIST: Roberto Parada
WRITER: Staff

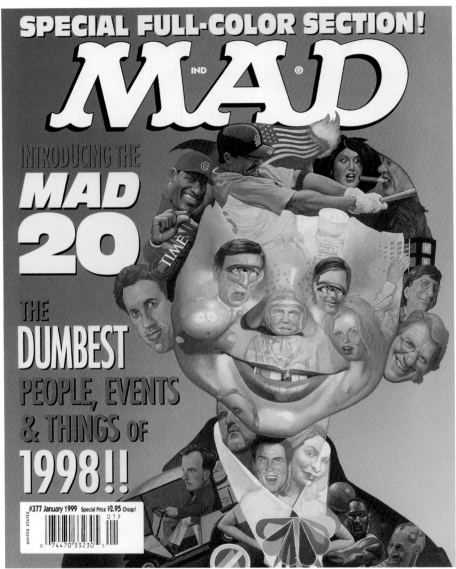

The premiere of the infamous "*MAD* 20." The cover by Roberto Parada was inspired by C. C. Beall Jr.'s classic cover for issue #39.

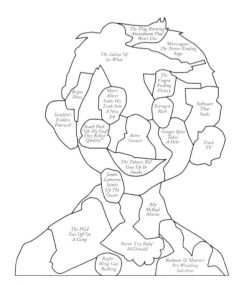

MAD #377 front cover key

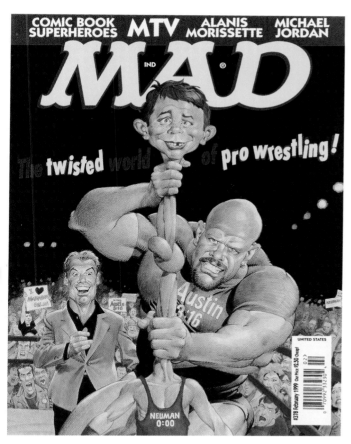

MAD #378
February 1999
ARTIST: Mort Drucker
WRITER: Staff

MAD #379
March 1999
ARTIST: Drew Struzan
WRITER: John Caldwell

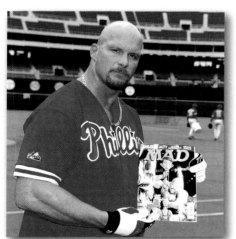

Stone Cold Steve Austin

MAD reader Tou-Liang Chang and Yo Yo Ma

Preliminary cover concept for MAD #379 by John Caldwell (left); preliminary cover rough by Nick Meglin (right)

MAD #380
April 1999
ARTIST: David O'Keefe
WRITER: Staff

A: Sculpted in clay, then photographed.

Q: In a first for *MAD,* how were Alex Trebek and Alfred presented on this cover?

▼ *MAD* #381
May 1999
ARTIST: Scott Bricher
WRITER: Staff

▶ *MAD* #382
June 1999
ARTIST: Mark Stutzman
WRITER: Don "Duck" Edwing

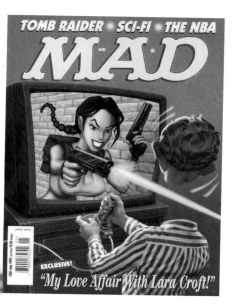

Views varied widely about the appeal of this cover. Some readers were put off by its grossness. Others complained that it wasn't gross enough. All in all, a mixture of ooze and aahs.

MAD #383

July 1999

ARTIST: Roberto Parada
WRITER: Staff

Because the editors were split on which of their ideas would make a more effective cover, they decided to use both, taking inspiration from the preliminary teaser poster (below) for *Star Wars Episode 1: The Phantom Menace* (1999). In actuality they printed two covers with the hope that rabid *Star Wars* fans would buy both. (They didn't.)

Preliminary cover concept for *MAD* #383 by Nick Meglin (top left); preliminary cover concept by Sam Viviano (top middle); preliminary cover concept by Sam Viviano (top right); preliminary cover sketch by Roberto Parada (bottom left); preliminary cover sketch by Roberto Parada (bottom right)

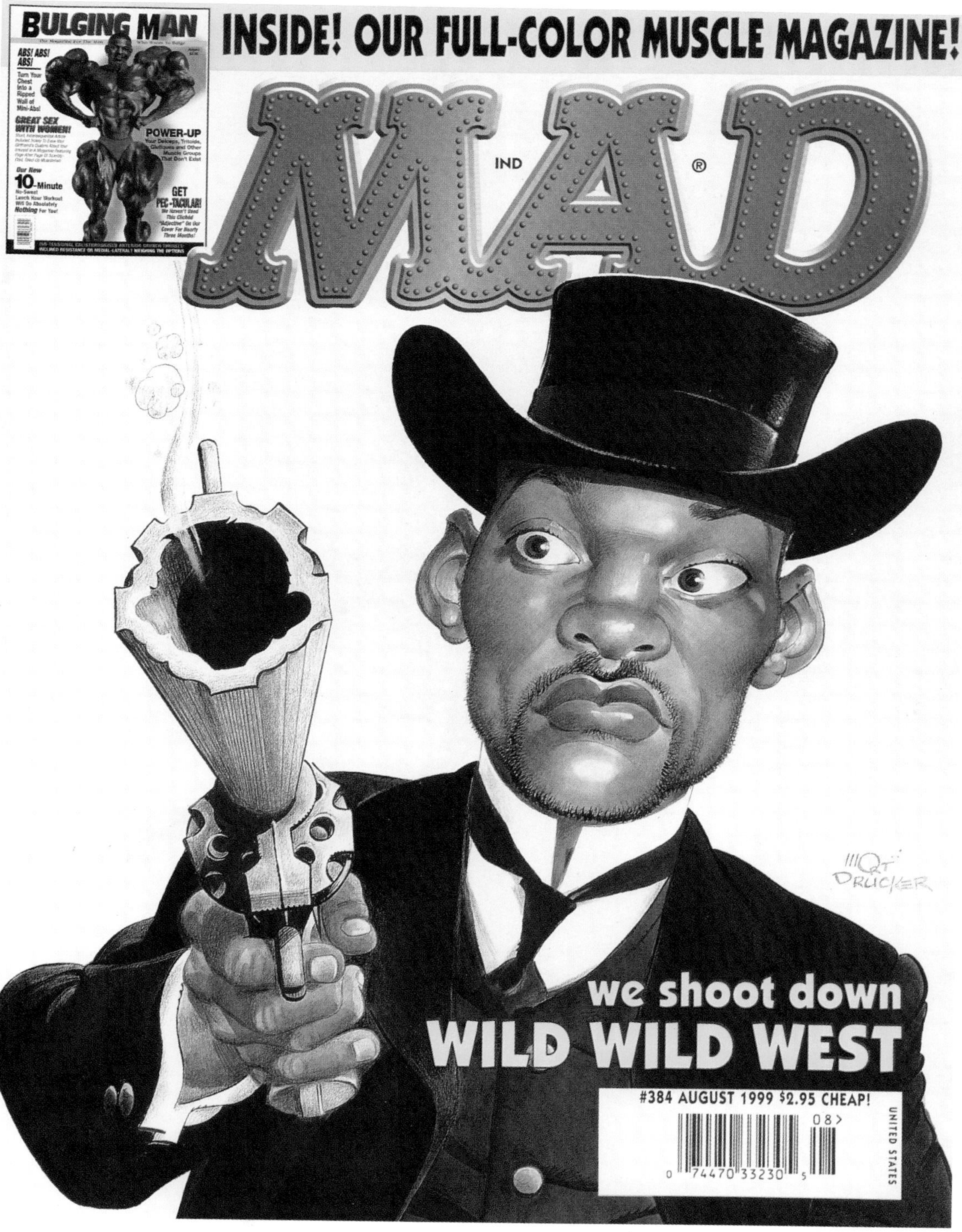
BULGING MAN
INSIDE! OUR FULL-COLOR MUSCLE MAGAZINE!
ABS! ABS! ABS!
POWER-UP
10-Minute
GET PEC-TACULAR!
MAD
IND
we shoot down
WILD WILD WEST
#384 AUGUST 1999 $2.95 CHEAP!
UNITED STATES

***MAD* #384**
August 1999
ARTIST: Mort Drucker
WRITER: Staff

With a brilliant execution by Mort Drucker, the shape of Alfred's head provides a barrel of laughs!

MAD #385
September 1999
ARTIST: Mark Stutzman
WRITER: Staff

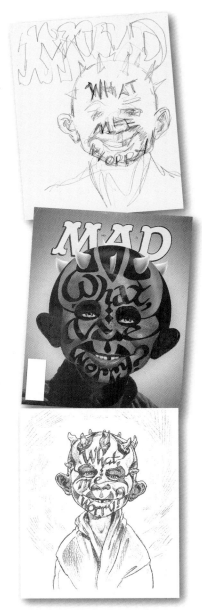

Preliminary cover concept for *MAD* #385 by Nick Meglin (top); preliminary computer cover comp by Sam Viviano (middle); preliminary cover sketch by Mark Stutzman (bottom)

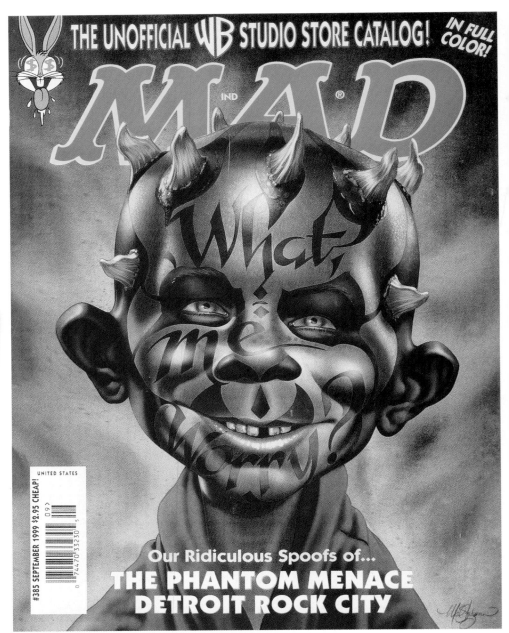

MAD is translated and published around the world in eleven international editions. Since humor and topical subject matter varies from country to country, *MAD*'s foreign publishers are allowed free editorial rein, and in most instances create their own covers best suited to their market; other times the artwork from the U.S. cover is modified and slightly adapted. Here we see Alfred as the villainous Darth Maul from *Star Wars Episode 1: The Phantom Menace,* as published in the United States and around the world.

Sweden

India

Germany

Finland

Brazil

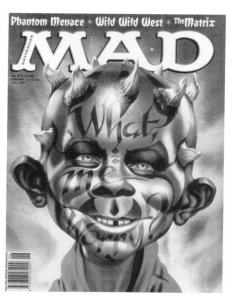

Australia

MAD #386
October 1999
ARTIST: James Warhola
WRITER: Staff

One hour after this issue went on sale, the *MAD* Web site had registered more than nine thousand hits. When all the votes were counted, the choice was rear-ending Pokémon with the dynamite schtick.

Special full-color insert! *plus*
BLAIR WITCH·BIG DADDY·SOUTH PARK·AMERICAN PIE

MAD

THE 20TH CENTURY—WHY IT SUCKED!

UNITED STATES

#387 NOVEMBER 1999 $2.95 CHEAP!

0 74470 33230 5

◀ **MAD #387**
November 1999
ARTIST: Joe DeVito
WRITER: Staff

▼ **MAD #388**
December 1999
ARTIST: Scott Bricher
WRITER: Peter Kuper

MAD
NOW Y2K COMPLIANT!

Puffy Combs
Ricky Martin
Spy vs. Spy
Dead People
...and More!

#388 DECEMBER 1999 $2.95 CHEAP!

Preliminary cover concept for
MAD #388 by Peter Kuper

Preliminary cover sketch for
MAD #387 by Joe DeVito

MAD #389

January 2000

ARTIST: Drew Friedman

WRITER: Staff

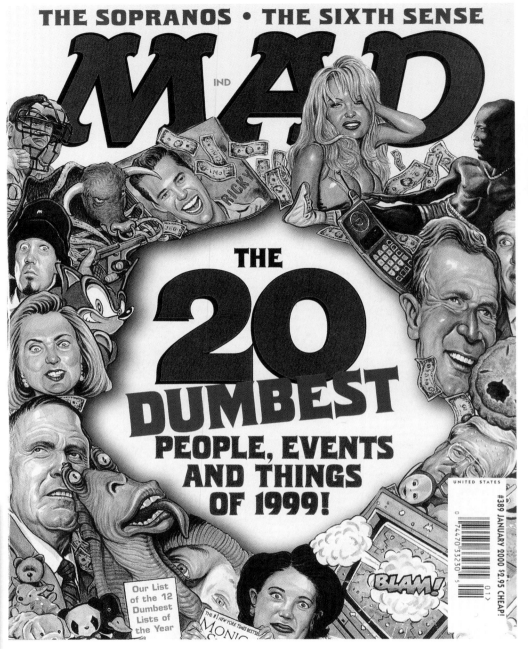

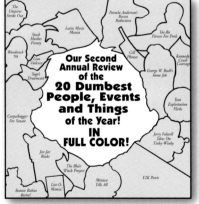

MAD #389 front cover key

MAD's first issue of the new millennium, featuring the second annual "20 Dumbest" honorees. (The first annual "20 Dumbest" honorees was #377.) This may be hard to swallow, but only one person made both covers—a dubious distinction at best.

▼ **MAD #390**
February 2000
ARTIST: Mark Fredrickson
WRITER: Peter Kuper

▶ **MAD #391**
March 2000
ARTIST: Richard Williams
WRITER: Staff

Preliminary cover concept for
MAD #390 by Peter Kuper

Harry Potter gets his comeuppance, the cover billboarding an eight-page parody within the magazine. Because of the popularity of the books with both teenage and adult readers, *MAD* chose this to be its first text piece spoofing a literary work—a real change for its subliterate editors.

Preliminary cover sketch for
MAD #391 by Richard Williams.
From the collection of Mike Gidwitz

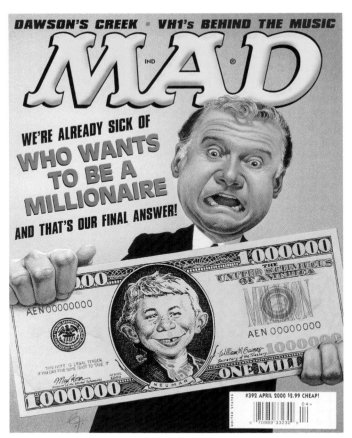

DAWSON'S CREEK · VH1's BEHIND THE MUSIC

WE'RE ALREADY SICK OF
WHO WANTS
TO BE A
MILLIONAIRE
AND THAT'S OUR FINAL ANSWER!

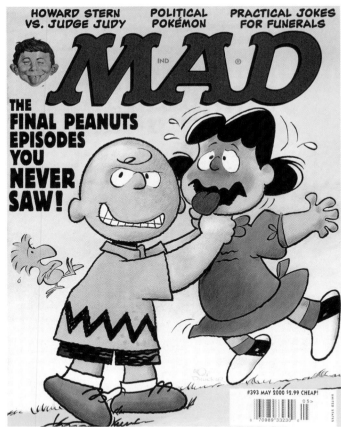

HOWARD STERN VS. JUDGE JUDY   POLITICAL POKÉMON   PRACTICAL JOKES FOR FUNERALS

THE FINAL PEANUTS EPISODES YOU NEVER SAW!

MAD #392
April 2000
ARTIST: C. F. Payne
WRITER: Staff

Cashing in on the Regis Philbin *Who Wants to Be a Millionaire?* phenomenon, *MAD* presents its final answer to the question: "Who is pictured on the million dollar bill?" Who else but Alfred E. Pluribus Neuman.

MAD #393
May 2000
ARTIST: Mort Drucker
WRITER: Staff

Preliminary cover concept for *MAD* #392 by John Ficarra (top left); preliminary cover rough by Sam Viviano (top middle); preliminary cover sketch by C. F. Payne (top right)

MAD reader Sali Riesterer and Regis Philbin

Preliminary cover concepts for *MAD* #393 by Sam Viviano

IN THIS ISSUE WE SOCK IT TO
POKÉMON ❖ "THE PRACTICE" ❖ THE CLASS OF 2000

MAD

UNITED STATES

#394 JUNE 2000 $2.99 CHEAP!
0 70989 33230 0

MAD #394
June 2000
ARTIST: Richard Williams
WRITER: Staff

The editors were blessed with a plethora of ideas for this cover, all dogs! But the marathon brainstorming session "may have been one of the most creative and funniest cover meetings we ever had," according to co-editor John Ficarra. The result was not one but two dog covers: this one, featuring the Pets.com sock puppet, as well as the cover for #397, featuring Alfred and the Taco Bell Chihuahua.

▲ Preliminary cover concepts for *MAD* #394 by Nick Meglin (top row); preliminary cover concepts by Sam Viviano (middle and bottom rows)

◀ Preliminary computer cover comps by Sam Vivano

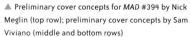

MAD #395
July 2000
ARTIST: James Bennett
WRITER: Don "Duck" Edwing

Forty years after its first election-year cover (#56), *MAD* again took aim at the presidential candidates. With this double-cover issue, readers had their choice of selecting their least-liked nominee. *MAD* was hoping that the choice, admittedly difficult, would tempt readers to buy both issues, or at the very least prompt a mass write-in vote for Alfred.

Artist/writer Don "Duck" Edwing. Photo by Irving Schild (October 1993)

Preliminary cover concepts for *MAD* #395 by Don "Duck" Edwing

Preliminary cover concepts by Sam Viviano

Preliminary computer cover comps by Sam Vivano

Preliminary cover sketches by James Bennett

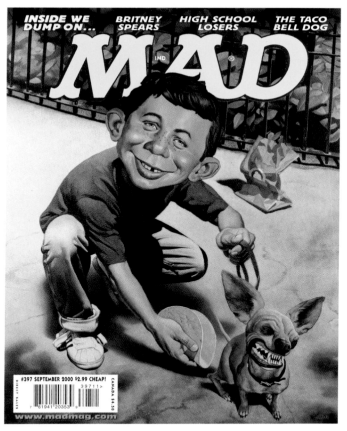

MAD #396
August 2000
ARTIST: Mort Drucker
WRITER: John Caldwell

Getting to the heart of the matter, *MAD* bypassed the boundaries of good taste, revealing the result of David Letterman's surgery. Lord only knows what *MAD* would have done if Letterman had undergone a hemorrhoid operation.

The issue inaugurated *MAD*'s *Worst Things About* feature, this one lambasting TV.

Artist/writer John Caldwell.
Photo by Irving Schild
(October 1993)

MAD #397
September 2000
ARTIST: Roberto Parada
WRITER: Staff

Preliminary cover concept for *MAD* #397 by Sam Viviano (left); preliminary cover sketch by Roberto Parada (right)

Preliminary cover concept for *MAD* #396 by John Caldwell (left); preliminary cover rough by Sam Viviano (middle); preliminary cover sketch by Mort Drucker (right)

MAD #398
October 2000
ARTIST: James Bennett
WRITER: Staff

Preliminary cover concept for *MAD* #398 by Sam Viviano (left); preliminary cover sketch by James Bennett (right)

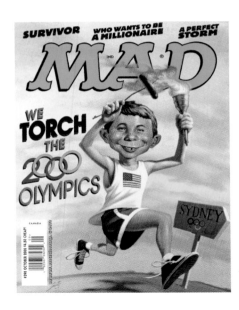

MAD #399
November 2000
ARTIST: ?
WRITER: ?

YOU BE THE EDITOR.

You've now looked at 398 *MAD* covers and learned the angst, twisted thinking, and stupidity that goes into deciding on a cover. As this book went to press, the *MAD* editors were just beginning work on the cover of issue #399. But, as always, there were problems, considerations, and disagreements over what the cover should be. Here's your chance to play *MAD* editor (though we can't imagine why anyone in their right mind would want to!). What cover would *you* come up with, given the following conditions:

MAD #399 will feature a satire of the movie *X-Men,* a parody of the MTV show *Total Request Live,* and possibly a takeoff of either HBO's *Sex in the City* or the movies *What Lies Beneath* and/or *Space Cowboys.*

X-Men is a huge summer hit, especially among males, who constitute 80 percent of *MAD*'s readership. The only problem is this issue will go on sale October 17, a full three months after the movie debuted. Will an *X-Men* cover look too dated? Or will the movie have enough "legs" to make an *X-Men* cover still effective?

Total Request Live is one of the highest-rated shows on MTV. It obviously attracts millions of young viewers, just the kind of people *MAD* is trying to attract. The show will air every day that this issue is on sale, so there is no problem about looking too dated with a *TRL* cover. The problem is that the show's host, Carson Daly, is not terribly recognizable to the broad spectrum of *MAD* readers. Do you run a *TRL*/Carson Daly cover and risk leaving behind a certain percentage of potential *MAD* readers?

Sex in the City is a very adult show that airs only on HBO, where its audience is much smaller than a network show. *What Lies Beneath* and *Space Cowboys* have yet to open to a national audience, but an early reviewer of *What Lies Beneath* has panned the movie. Do you wait until the very last minute and see how these films do, with the chance that if they both bomb, you have nothing for the cover of the issue and only a week to come up with something?

Or . . . there is always a generic Alfred gag kicking around the office. One idea in particular (see below) in many ways is a "classic Alfred gag." But some staff members have argued that it's not sexy enough and that it may be "too highbrow."

These were our choices, now they're your choices! Which one do *you* go with? Or none of the above.

And you thought being one of "The Usual Gang of Idiots" was easy!

Preliminary cover sketch by Sam Viviano

MAD #400
December 2000
PHOTOMOSAIC: Robert Silvers
WRITER: Staff

The idea for this cover had been floating around the *MAD* offices for several years. It wasn't until the editors were working on this book and realized the timing of its publication with the magazine's four hundredth issue that it was able to all come together. This incredible Photomosaic by Robert Silvers was also turned into a signed limited-edition lithograph by the Warner Bros. Studio Stores.

INDEX of *MAD* Cover Creators